CW01661919

Ghosts of Rosevear

and The Wreck of the Nancy Packet

by

Todd Stevens & Edward Cumming

For Ruth & Ian.

Ed Cumming

Front and rear cover picture - ***The Nancy Packet*** **by James Gillray Published by Robert Wilkinson 1784. Engraving, Etching, Stipple. (Courtesy of the Isles of Scilly Museum after Mr & Mrs Browning donated their copy of this extremely rare print to that institution. Amazingly, this remarkable generosity was at the exact moment in time when the authors were seeking the use of a colour copy of the picture for this publication during the winter of 2007-08)**

Satirist James Gillray was an 18th century English draughtsman and engraver who, almost single handedly, invented the genre of British political caricature. The front cover of this book was one of only two attempts Gillray made at branching out with his talents into a more serious subject matter. This wonderfully evocative print, Gillray's depiction of the *Nancy* packet disaster, was criticised at the time as being overly melancholy.

Acknowledgements

Gibson's of Scilly
Chris Peat
Rev. Dr. James Jack
Mike Fardell
Steve Chesire
Steve Sherris
Captain Roger Abbott
Vivian Burgess
Andrea Cordani
Glynis Greenman
Alan Read
Jean Sutton
Father Guy Scott
Alfred Trenear
Amanda Martin
Barbara Simpson
Helena Wakefield
Carmen Stevens
Barbara Cumming
Phillip Roberts
James Fletcher
Paul Stevens
Terry Hiron
Chris Hall
Danni Hudson
Robin Burrows
Mr & Mrs Browning
Trinity House
Institute of Civil Engineers
Harry Ransom Humanities Research Centre
(The University of Texas at Austin USA)
The Isles of Scilly Museum

Published by
Todd Stevens & MIBEC Enterprises

First Edition 2008

Formatting and layout by Carmen & Todd Stevens
St Mary's Isles of Scilly

Printed by
R Booth Ltd
Penryn
Cornwall
TR10 9HH

ISBN: 0-9542104 5 X
ISBN: 978 09542104 5 8

Contents

Section (1)

1. Western Rocks
2. Rosevear and the Bishop
3. The Lighthouse Builder's Tale
4. Leaving Rosevear

Section (2)

1. Miss Brown
2. Ann Cargill
3. Child of Misfortune
4. *"Eastward Ho!"*
5. Mr L
6. The *Nancy* Packet
7. St Helena
8. Scilly, Anvil of the Atlantic
9. Self Preservation
10. Forlorn Hope
11. Cargill's Clay
12. Re-committal at Old Town

Section (3)

1. Aftermath
2. The Braithwaites
3. Eureka
4. Diving Rosevear Ledges
5. Guns and Anchors
6. Old Town Revisited
7. The Grave on Rosevear

Poem Lullaby of Rosevear

Introduction

The authors do not believe in ghosts, however, the tale of the wreck of the East India packet ship *Nancy* is inextricably linked with a legendary haunting of Rosevear island where the ship was lost. As a result, the authors decided to embrace the legend and present it alongside the factual story with which it is associated; its inclusion has made the book all the more fascinating.

This publication is divided into three distinct parts:

Section (1) is about Rosevear island, its legend, and the unique events that surrounded the workforce who built the Bishop Rock Lighthouse.

Section (2) covers the life of actress and singer Ann Cargill which includes the fate of Captain John Haldane and the packet ship *Nancy*

Section (3) relates to diving and the modern day search for the wrecksite.

All verses contained between the chapters were taken from two separate poems, both of which were written about the *Nancy* packet disaster. One of these poems was written by an unknown author contemporary with the wreck. The other poem, after comparing it to the works of popular Scillonian poet Robert Maybee, the authors believe this to be his work and composed sometime in the mid to late victorian era. Both poems can be found in their entirity at the back of the book.

This book is a collaboration between two, similar minded, enthusiastic diver/shipwreck historians. Written by Todd Stevens but predominantly researched by Edward Cumming.

All photographs and illustrations by Todd and Carmen Stevens unless stated otherwise.

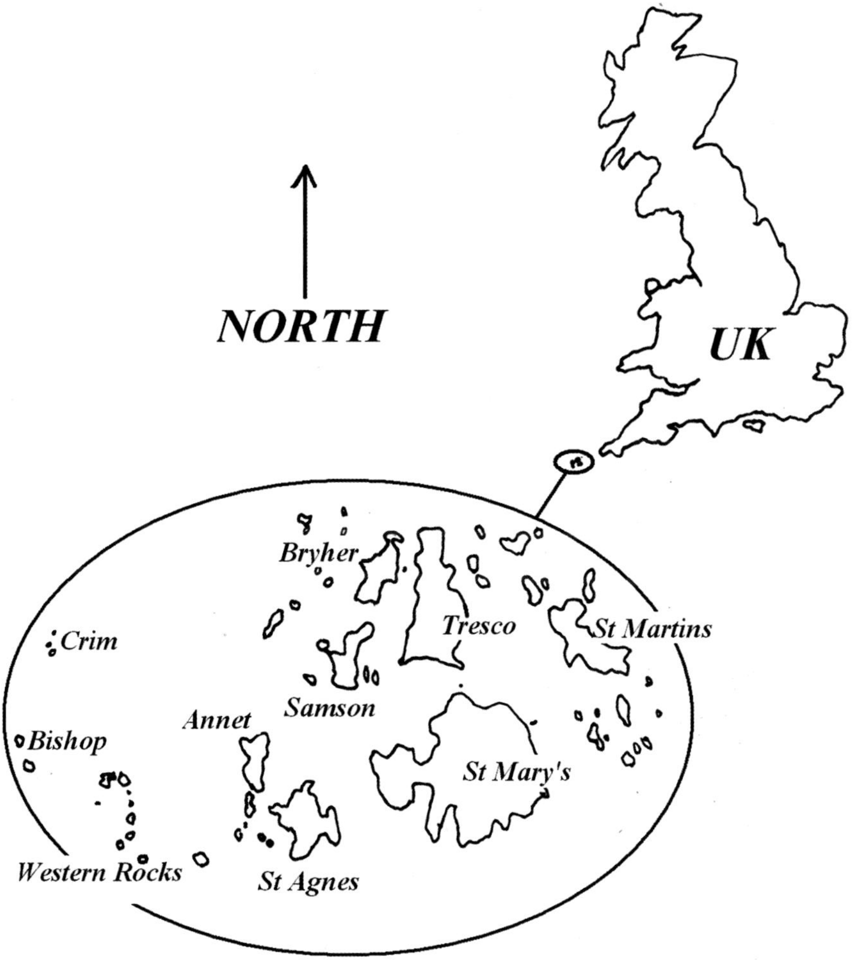

The Isles of Scilly

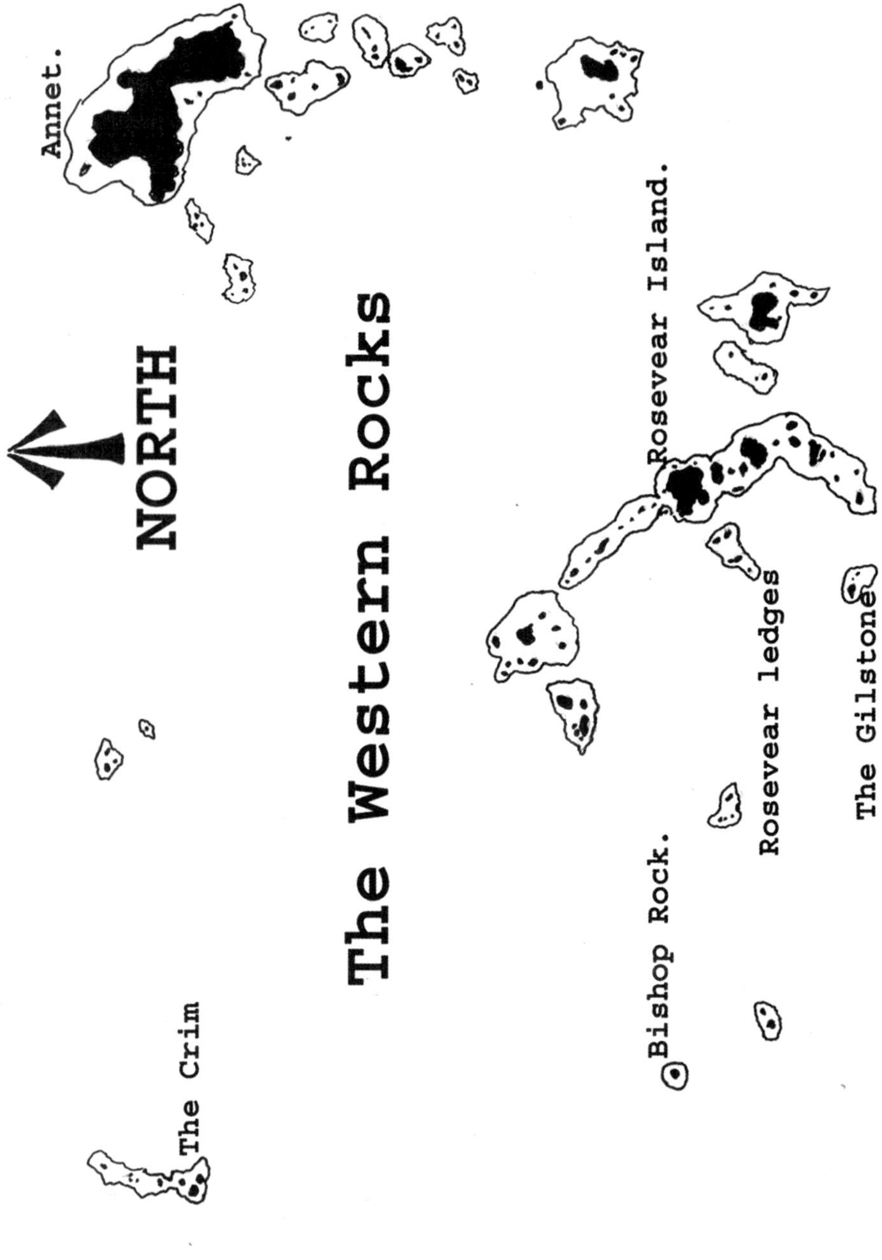
The Western Rocks
NORTH
Annet.
Rosevear Island.
Rosevear ledges
The Gilstone
Bishop Rock.
The Crim

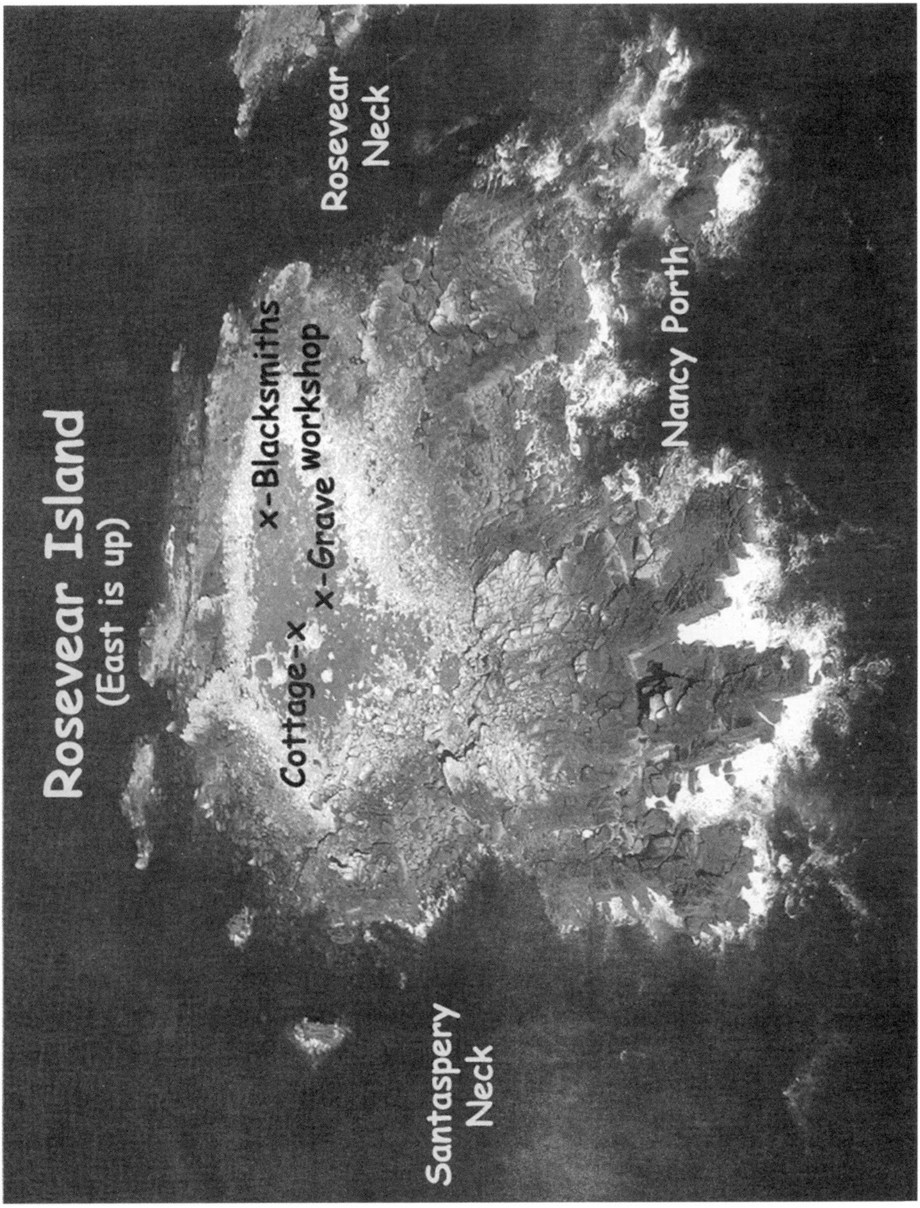

Original Photograph by Chris Peat
(Santaspery Neck is North)

Cargill, who did rival Venus,
now alas! will charm no more.
Each rose and lily now is faded,
wrecked near Scilly's fatal shore.
Robert Maybee

SECTION (1)

1. Western Rocks

Early eighteenth century German copperplate print of the *Association* disaster
(Courtesy of Terry Hiron)

It was once written that all ghosts, ghouls, goblins, phantoms and unholy apparitions were charmed from, cast in a spell, or otherwise conjured away from Scilly some time ago in the islands long and distant past. Certainly, author H.J. Whitfield wrote this of the Isles of Scilly: *"There is not, I believe, a satisfactory ghost in any one of them".* Nevertheless, an awful lot of time has passed with many tragedies having occurred since that time. Most of these disasters have happened at sea in shipwrecks around the peripheral rocks of Scilly; away from the view of the main inhabited islands. An almost incalculable number of lives have been lost as a result. As any informed islander will convey, the vast majority of shipwrecks at Scilly occurred among the Western Rocks; a vast area between the Isle of Annet and the Bishop Rock Lighthouse. A short flick through accounts of local shipwreck losses will give the reader some idea of the scale of horrific deaths suffered amidst these terrible rocks. Disaster and tragedy inevitably spark tales of spectres and supernatural occurrences although, strangely enough, very few ghost stories appear to have been attributed to any of these human tragedies. However, one particular legendary haunting will be dealt with in this book.

Anyone who visits the infamous Western Rocks of Scilly generally returns with an opinion about the area. Many find their experience to have been mystical, eerie or otherwise disconcerting. Certainly, when one is among the Western Rocks on a calm day, especially around dusk when the resident seals are whining, it is an experience capable of unnerving many. Even some locals will rarely venture out that way and certainly not alone. As active divers we, the authors, know fellow sportsmen who will avoid visiting certain shipwrecks in that area if at all possible, for as they tend to put it: *"that wreck always gives me the heebee geebee's".*

On any typical calm day in the season, local tour boats will venture out to this part of the islands. Many of these vessels have a knowledgeable local skipper, able to talk to his passengers at length about any given rock and just what disaster occurred there. The horrifying banter, conveyed to the customers during the journey, will go something like the following. We pick up the trip as the boat heads west, passing around the uninhabited island of Annet: *"The narrow stretch of water we're passing along now is called the Neck of Hellweathers"* says the Skipper. "*See that large rock over there to the right, well that is where Captain Dow and only one other man were saved from the wreck of the Thomas W Lawson. Everyone else perished in the disaster in1907 over there between Shag rock and the outer Ranney Rocks beyond."*

The tour boat then makes its way towards the more distant Western Rocks. Once there, no doubt the passengers will be told the story of how, out of over three hundred souls, not one person survived the wreck of the Dutch East India ship *Hollandia* in 1743, and how divers found a mound of silver treasure down below on the wreck site. Eventually, the boat arrives alongside a long natural barrier of granite outcrops, in the region of Jacky's Rock, where 60 lives were lost in the steamer *Thames* in 1841. The boatman, before moving on, points towards Jacky's Rock and describes the scene as it was reported in the newspapers of the time: *"Here is where, with a tremendous sea running, the steamer Thames went to pieces. Of the 60 victims, some managed to clamber aboard floating wreckage and made for the uninhabited island of Rosevear. Unfortunately, by the time they reached the shore, they were so exhausted they could not climb the rocks and were drowned in the surf; only one survived."*

Amazingly, two years after the *Thames* was wrecked, a ship called the *Nickerie* struck the other side of the very same rock. The attempt at survival by the crew of the *Nickerie,* reads almost identical to that of the *Thames*. Then, with the passengers in the tour boat expressing their shock or pity towards the victims of these two similar disasters, the boat moves off towards the south. In passing only a short distance it moves over numerous other shipwrecks, one of which, the *Prinses Maria,* is only pointed out due to the treasure reputed to have been on board when she sank. No mention is made of the many crewmen that died that night in 1686. The vessel then passes Rosevear island. As it turns west into the Rosevear Neck on the south side of the island, many interesting historical facts are conveyed about that small piece of land surrounded by water. Occasionally the legend of the island being haunted is also briefly mentioned as the boat makes its way out and on towards the Gilstone reef.

Once alongside the Gilstone the boat is brought to a halt, and as close as is safely possible alongside this infamous rock. *"Here we have the Gilstone"* says the skipper continuing with his guided tour with perhaps a little more enthusiasm than before; and why not, apart from the *Titanic,* the wreck of *HMS Association* has arguably become *the* most famous disaster at sea of all time. The skipper continues; *"This is where Admiral Sir Cloudisley Shovell and over 600 sailors met their gruesome end. A further 1000 souls were lost in three other ships of the same fleet on other rocks hereabouts. All this happened in one fateful October night in 1707".* A fantastic history lesson of the tragedy and its aftermath then follows. Then conveyed to the interested sightseer, is the tale of the ensuing treasure hunt that still goes on to this very day.

Eventually, the tour boat moves off to other wreck sites on its melancholy journey, the skipper telling of disaster after disaster. *SS Schiller,* over 300 souls lost; *Zeelilie,* 300 people lost; *Antonious; Douro*; *Falkland;* the list is endless. Any one of these events has more than enough real tragedy to initiate a ghostly tale doing the rounds but strangely very few have come to pass.
A sad account of what it is like to be amongst the Western Rocks when tragedy strikes, was recorded by one of the Bishop Rock Lighthouse keepers, captured for all time in a letter to his wife. It was written as a direct result of the loss of the *SS Schiller* in 1875. The man was clearly distressed:

"Dear wife, *Bishop Rock May 10th*

With heart sick grief I write to inform you of the dreadful wreck that has happened here, less than half a mile inside of us, on Friday inst. I had been on watch up to eight pm, when I was relieved by the man on duty whilst our principal keeper was on shore, but seeing the fog setting in I still kept at the lantern and ordered the bell to be set going at 8.40pm - fog very thick. I timed the bell properly at 6 strokes per minute, and saw that all was right. I left the lantern at 10pm and went to my bunk, but could not sleep. At 11.35pm William Mortimer (fellow keeper) came running down and called to me and said he could see a vessel on the rocks. I jumped up and went out to the parapet without stopping to dress, and saw the masthead and starboard light of a large steamer. She was burning blue lights and firing off guns and rockets. She seemed to be sinking. The last gun was fired at 1.30am on the 8th inst. I relieved G Gould at 4.00am.

Fog again raised at 6.00am and I could then just see the top of the mast of the vessel out of the water. We could count about 26 people in the rigging. I could see one lady in the lee side of the rigging with two males beside her. She was in a sitting position, I should think lashed. It was a dreadful sight. At about 7am the mast fell and I suppose everyone perished but I still hope a few or some might be saved. On Sunday three bodies floated past us, and this afternoon more have passed close by to us. No one knows what was felt in the house by all hands to see so many of our dear fellow creatures suffering and dying so near to us. Their sufferings must have been severe, for it was a cold drizzling rain all night, wind WSW. I think you had better take this letter, together with my compliments to John Banfield, Lloyds Agent. I remain your affectionate husband,
James Daniel.

Imagine now, having been told some of the shipwreck stories earlier described, then having to live isolated on a tiny spit of land amidst that history of tragedies past. Here you reside, day after day, cut off from the outside world without communication, power, or any other comforts of modern day life. Under such circumstances, even the most sceptical of people would eventually begin to understand why others have found the atmosphere of this area rather disconcerting. They may even admit to having experienced something strange or unusual; and, as you will soon read, the circumstances described immediately above did take place.

The tragic disaster and related events recorded in this publication, also took place among the Western Rocks of Scilly. Some of those described in the following chapters, referred to as living and working in this isolated place, experienced at first hand circumstances like those described above. As a result, they actually went on to believe that they witnessed many strange phenomena. These were normal everyday people but they were so affected by their experiences that the ghost stories they conveyed still live on in the minds of many current inhabitants of Scilly. The shipwreck behind the tale, however, has been all but forgotten; strange considering this particular shipwreck is surrounded by a fabulous and romantic history of a once very famous individual. Rosevear island is central to this now mythical haunting that has stood the test of time, with the island being the supposed link between the living and the dead. Many will say *"But it's just a tale"* however, on that tiny island and its surrounding reefs there still remains tantalizing evidence of how this legendary ghost story came about. To further substantiate the beliefs of many, that there is indeed something rather peculiar about the Western Rocks of Scilly, there have been sufficient enough incidents as to warrant them being reported in newspapers of the time. Two accounts found in the Times Newspaper alone, were of men having strange experiences while working out among the Western Rocks. As recently as November 6th 1947 the Times reports that a mason, Mr Prowse of Penzance, who after trying to perform his job, was recovered by boat from the Western Rocks in a distressed state of mind: *"when he stepped ashore this afternoon, he seemed to go to pieces."* The cause of his anguish is unclear but a much earlier report may throw a little light upon the subject. This next report, also in the Times, this time on January 29th 1913, refers to men who worked on Rosevear island and who built the Bishop Rock Lighthouse. It states that an iron anvil weighing some one and one half hundred weight, seemingly moved out of a secure position of its own accord and that: "*the workmen attributed the occurrence to supernatural agency, and they were with difficulty persuaded to return to the spot".* This report clearly shows the men were in a distressed state of mind similar to that of Mr Prowse.

One strange and unexplained occurrence on its own, is not enough to make a group of grown workmen behave in such a manner as to need coaxing back to their place of work. This must surely mean that a culmination of similar unexplained events, leading up to the reported incident, must have taken place. One of those who encouraged his colleagues back to work was engineer James Nicholas Douglass. James was born in Middlesex in 1826 and those who felt it a privilege to have worked under him, referred to him as *Cap'n Jim.*

The Douglass family built many lighthouses around the coasts of England, Wales, Scotland, Ireland and France. Fortunately for us James kept a record of his working life and this, aided by his wife Mary, was later turned into a book by Thomas Williams and published in 1900.

Described many times by his peers as the *indefatigable engineer*, James Douglass was known to be a forthright, honest, hardworking leader of men. Certainly not, one would think, the type of man to believe in the supernatural. However, reading through the record of his life's work, a good insight is gained into the building of the Bishop Rock Lighthouse and events that occurred on Rosevear Island. One or two paragraphs even refer to the existence of a haunting: *"The workmen, mostly Cornish, who lived on Rosevear, had all the superstition of their race; and scarcely one of them, though he would have faced, bravely enough, any tangible danger, cared to stay on the island, for fear of ghosts".* Clearly these men collectively believed the Island to be haunted. The above record also goes on to describe a particular incident that involved the resident Head Blacksmith. This, however, will be dealt with in the next chapter.

James Douglass
Courtesy of the Institute of Civil Engineers

The Bishop Rock Lighthouse in a howling gale
Circa 1900.

All night the booming minute-gun
Had peeled along the deep'
And mournfully the rising sun,
Looked o'er the tide worn steep.
Unknown author

2. Rosevear and the Bishop

The ruins of the construction workers cottage on Rosevear island
Viewed looking southwest

Rosevear island, where the construction workers once lived and worked, is the last landfall in the Atlantic Ocean between England and America. It is a mere speck of land of about eight hundred feet long by seven hundred feet wide; its highest point standing no more than forty feet above high tide level. The name Rosevear derives from Cornish, a feminine word meaning *'From the Moorland'.*

Although the island is a bleak and lonely place, it is the only bastion among the Western Rocks to harbour a meagre capping of earth supporting some hardy green vegetation. The tree mallows growing there are lush, turning the top of the island deep green in colour and making it a striking sight when viewed at close quarter from a boat. Perhaps this is from where the island's other name *'Roche Verde',* originates. Rosevear is the only island among the Western Rocks that manages to sustain this modicum of plant life. It is a place where one can expect to find only squawking gulls and whining seals for company. Puffins and many other seabirds also frequent the area during warmer months. There are no beaches around the island only sloping granite bedrock; sheer sided rocky carns and tumble down boulders all reaching down into the sea. Apart from two narrow waterways, *Santaspery Neck* and *Rosevear Neck*, which run to the north and south of the island respectively, none of the features of Rosevear appear to be identified or associated with any given names. However, on the western side of the island is a small but prominent bay. This bay, we the authors have elected to call *'Nancy Porth'*, the reasons for which will become obvious later in the book.

For such a tiny place, Rosevear is extensively scarred with evidence of man's relatively recent interaction with the island; the remains of a modest cottage being the most prominent. However, there are also two large flat and level granite platforms; one is south of the cottage; the other east. The one to the south served as the floor to the blacksmith's workshop; the one to the east is probably the foundation of the tool shed. There are also other features just east of the cottage which also served as out-buildings. From the position of the Blacksmith's workshop there is evidence of where a walkway, probably constructed of wood, ran in a southerly direction down to the sea. This is visible by way of deep cut-outs into the granite, or flattened areas of rock. There are even steps down to the water at the end of the walkway.There are also many other features to be found; many are of iron fixings or cuts and holes in the granite. In fact there are too many features to list them all here.

The only recorded human habitation on the island occurred in the mid nineteenth century when, in 1847, work began on a project to build the very first lighthouse on the Bishop Rock. To aid this work some wooden shacks were erected on Rosevear for the purpose. It is unclear whether the first workmen actually lived on the Island. However, logistics of the project suggest that they must have done.

The Bishop Rock is a small wave-washed islet some two miles

northwest of Rosevear island and the lighthouse initially constructed there was made almost entirely of iron. Unfortunately, during the great storm of 1850, this lighthouse was washed away by the sea; as reported by the Proceedings of the Institute of Civil Engineers in 1892: "*There* it (Bishop Rock) *is exposed to the full force of the Atlantic waves rolling in from an unbroken stretch of 3,600 nautical miles. With this small base a lighthouse has been erected. (sic) Very wonderful are the force of the waves during violent storms. The first tower, erected by Mr N. Douglass, was an open structure composed of wrought and cast iron columns supporting a lantern 94ft above high water mark. After surmounting all obstacles the tower was completed after four years work, and left during the winter of 1849 to wait for its lantern apparatus. But a heavy storm on the night of February 5, 1850, snapped the columns, and carried away the upper solid portion of the structure, thus showing the waves must have flowed bodily over the rock at a height of over 90ft above high water mark*" Similarly, being in such an exposed position, the wooden shacks erected on Rosevear did not last for very long either.

Later that same year Nicholas Douglass, the very same engineer who built the first iron lighthouse, was charged with building a new granite replacement. Granite buildings, replacing the tumbled down wooden shacks previously employed on the island, were also constructed. During this second project the workforce certainly took up residence on Rosevear, since this was recorded by Thomas Williams in 1900: "*During the summer months the supervising engineers and the working staff resided on Rosevear, an otherwise uninhabited island or rock, of small area. Here they were within a couple of miles off the Bishop, could clearly see, in ordinary states of the atmosphere, what probability there was of effecting a landing thereon, and quickly reach that site when there proved to be the least chance of working there. But the life on Rosevear was often one of extreme discomfort and misery.*"

James and William, the sons of Nicholas Douglass, were the chief engineers on site. Although similar in technical experience, James was slightly older than his brother William. Both men were extremely professional so there was no sibling rivalry. Instead, drawing on each other's skills, together they successfully managed the project and its workforce. This coalition was also extremely necessary, as naturally one man would occasionally need to leave the job in the hands of the other. Work started in 1852 and their reconstructed lighthouse wasn't completed until 1858. During that time James did in fact leave the project in William's capable hands for a combined total of over two years.

Only those who actually performed the work could fully appreciate the trials these men faced during the project. Nevertheless, one can easily imagine a high and wild sea encroaching on the small dwelling on Rosevear and even swamping it at times. After the sea had done this once too often, the men were forced to pile up large boulders at strategic places around the island, in order to protect themselves and their buildings from the sea.

These men were extremely tough individuals who were willing to place their very lives on the line. During stormy weather, sometimes for days on end, the men huddled inside the buildings for fear of being injured by falling rocks and stones that were carried in by the force of the waves. This problem was expressed at a dinner at the Institute of Civil Engineers 1892: *"When we read of limpets and stones weighing two and a half ounces being deposited 143ft above high water mark by the force of the waves, we may well commend the bravery and daring of the engineers who had charge of the construction and who dwell amid such surroundings".* Moreover, eminent geologist Samuel Joseph Mackie, after speaking to James Douglas, wrote the following passage in his 1858 report '*The Geology of the Isles of Scilly*', explaining the awesome power of the sea around Scilly: *"When lodging on Rosevear Island, to superintend the works connected with the Bishop Rock Lighthouse, he (*James Douglass*) had known blocks of granite twenty tons in weight, to be moved some distance by the sea".* A case showing the dangers of the sea overwhelming Rosevear island can also be found in references to the wreck of the steamer *Thames*. The day after the wreck some local boats went out to Rosevear where they were amazed to find a man awaiting rescue after having spent the night inside a barrel. In the Isles of Scilly Museum publication No. 9, 1973, labourer and popular local poet Robert Maybee explains in his memoirs how this man had: *"found a cask of porter that had been washed ashore from the wreck. He knocked the end of it in with a stone letting the porter run away, and rolled the cask up to the highest part of the island, where the sea could not wash it away."*

Rosevear was in fact the least of their worries, as the men faced greater perils on the Bishop Rock itself. As with any dangers faced by the team, the Douglass brothers would lead by example. Biographer Thomas Williams records many of the trials they faced but the following gives us an idea as to how lighthouse building was just a horrendous way to make a living: *"Then, after the building operations were commenced, there was a particular gully in which a party of masons, lead, of course, by Douglass, had to set the lowest stones of the work; when someone placed above them on watch would shout that there was a big sea coming; and suddenly; would burst upon them a tremendous wave by which they were immersed to a depth of a dozen feet, they clinging, meanwhile, to two iron stanchions fixed to the rock, and emerging at last breathless, and sometimes utterly exhausted, with the prospect of a similar experience shortly afterwards".*

If the men had managed to stay on the rock, they emerged battered and bruised: *"the men at such times throwing themselves down and clinging to one another, for support, with a grip so intense as sometimes to cause flesh wounds."*

Naturally there were pleasant experiences to be had during the project as well. For instance there were accomplished musicians among the men; James Douglass being one of them. When the weather was bad, they sat in the cottage and played for each other. During a sustained calm spell of weather they even played to some invited guests. Williams wrote: *"On one memorable occasion invitations were received, by dwellers on the other islands, from the officers and men at Rosevear, to a grand ball. The sheds were all cleared of their contents, brilliantly illuminated, and decorated with bunting, and, at the expected hour, the visitors arrived in innumerable boats. Dancing was kept up until early morning. When guests rowed back in the moonlight to the accompaniment of the barrack band, led by James Douglass, who played well on the Flute."*

Locals were not only invited onto Rosevear merely to party and enjoy themselves, as many Islanders were employed on the project. Local poet Robert Maybee was just one of many: *"In 1855 I engaged to work on the Trinity works, to build the Lighthouse on the Bishop Rock. It was a very pleasant summer, and I was much pleased with my employment."* Maybee initially worked for one year, helping to build the second lighthouse, but he was to return a year later to complete a further *"five years"* work on the project. Some of his time was spent on Rat Island where the granite was dressed before shipping out to the Western Rocks.

As with the first iron structure, the second lighthouse, now built of granite, was later damaged by the sea as reported by the Institute of Civil Engineers: *"The second tower which was of solid granite, very carefully and laboriously constructed, and whose focal plane was raised to over 110ft above high water mark, showed further proof of the extraordinary power of the waves. A 5cwt bell used as a warning in foggy weather, which was securely fastened 100ft above the sea, was torn from its supports during a storm and washed away. In the tower also such severe vibration was caused by the waves that the solid granite was found to be cracked several feet above high water. So severe was the strain put upon the structure that, after iron internal diagonal ties had been found to be of no avail."*

Older and wiser the Douglass brothers returned to Rosevear in

1882 to strengthen the structure still further. An after dinner speech at the Trinity House Annual Banquet in 1885 records the work: *"With regard to our work of last year, the principle and most interesting work has been the strengthening of the Bishop Rock Lighthouse which is in an exceedingly exposed position, and within reach of the tide. The work was commenced in 1882. The old tower is being encased from base to cornice with new masonry, and the whole structure carried up to 32ft above its present height. The situation renders the work difficult, but it is to be hoped that in the course of the next year it will be finished".* Finally completed in 1887, this work had in fact taken a further two years; hence five in total.

When all is said and done the project had been a great success, with everyone involved returning home safely; and this from a workplace described by Trinity House as: *"at all times dangerous, and frequently of great peril."* Perceiving such circumstances, they then went on to show their gratitude to the men in charge for ensuring the job had progressed though to completion: *"without loss of life, or the occurrence of any accident of a serious nature."* The men's state of mind is not mentioned.

Natural occurrences and dangers aside, none could have guessed at the unique circumstances that transpired out in that desolate place, or the *"supernatural agency"* these men believed they were experiencing and later relayed. With such hardy men residing on the island of Rosevear, it is hard to believe that they would even entertain notions of the existence of ghosts. However, people in the Victorian era were fascinated with the supernatural and even openly embraced it. It is hardly surprising that, as a result, there have been more reports of supernatural occurrences during the Victorian era than in any other period in British history. Regardless of this, for the Rosevear haunting to have been perpetuated by a society as small as the one at Scilly, a society aware of the hardiness and integrity of the men working on the lighthouse project, then the story can only have been reinvigorated, if not started, by those same hardy workmen. Part of the local legend has it that the ghost is said to have resurfaced when a member of the workforce, possibly James Douglass, made a macabre discovery whilst preparing an area of ground in order to grow some vegetables. According to Thomas Williams, in his book The Life of Sir James Nicholas Douglass, the men did indeed successfully grow vegetables on Rosevear: *"Frequently, for considerable periods, the lighthouse builders were shut off by rough weather from all communications with the other islands; and, on more than one occasion when their provisions gave out, were glad to satisfy the cravings of hunger by eating limpets. In fine weather, however, they caught plenty of fish, generally in nets set at night, and at suitable seasons of the year had an abundance of wild birds, chiefly Puffins, eggs; while the vegetables which they grew in the crevices of the rock were noted for their size and excellence".*

Whilst known records fail to show any extraordinary or macabre discoveries being made regarding the above vegetable plot, another passage from the same source as above does make reference to an unexplained incident; an odd event experienced by the Head Blacksmith who was regularly left alone on Rosevear island. It is interesting to note that, whilst the reference gives no indication to the "macabre discovery" it fits well with another part of the local legend, as the ghost of Rosevear is supposed to be that of a woman humming a lullaby: *"On one occasion, a Blacksmith, heard strains of beautiful music, and looked for the boats which he first thought must be bringing his comrades back, but none were visible; whence he knew that the music was not of this world".* Whilst this reference further substantiates the belief that a ghost existed, the legend states that the men simultaneously shared an experience of hearing a woman singing. Possibly this is mere local embellishment of the above reference; like a rolling snowball the tale gathers material as it traverses through successive generations. However, we must not forget that quotes already discussed, taken from very different sources, have a similar collective theme when referring to the supernatural i.e. *"the workmen attributed"* written in the Times Newspaper; and the "*scarcely a man* " statement written in the life of James Nicholas Douglass.

The Blacksmith's daily anguish obviously fuelled thoughts of the supernatural among the workmen on Rosevear, having a detrimental effect on their state of mind, especially whenever dusk fell over the islands. If one considers the effects of isolation, often referred to as *cabin fever*, and then spice the equation with a macabre discovery, one is left with the perfect recipe for the resulting *"supernatural agency"*.

A couple of questions now spring to mind: did the workmen have previous knowledge of the legend before work started on Rosevear? And: how has a haunting on such a remote island been kept alive for so long? The answers to both these questions lie in the nature of island life.

In somewhere as small as Scilly, life is such that every incident is conveyed to every individual, so too are any local myths, tales and legends to anyone residing on the islands for any length of time. The workforce employed in constructing the lighthouse was understandably quite large. In fact these men, along with their families, increased the population of Scilly by almost two hundred during the lighthouse-building project. This was an overall population increase of about ten percent. Therefore their interaction with the locals must have been on a huge scale. In fact, a quick look at the records show that James Douglass, one of the men central to events on Rosevear island, is a typical case in example. James married into an old and distinguished Scillonian family. He even took his wife's name out of respect and changed his surname to James Nicholas Tregarthen-Douglass. He then set up home with his new wife on the islands during the project. Workmen like James Douglass, who interacted with the locals, must have heard about the legend.

With Scilly being a tiny close knit community, all it would take is one single workman to state that he had experienced something strange on Rosevear for his story to permeate throughout the islands within days. Human nature would then have the whole community discussing the subject of the supernatural and relaying their own individual experiences to each other. Many local men were also employed on the project and their experiences would certainly have made it back to the other islands very quickly indeed. As a consequence, the ghost story would have become the talk of the islands. It is therefore reasonable to assume that the haunting was to the forefront of people's minds for quite a sustained period of time, especially while people continued to reside on the island in question. Given all the above, it was inevitable that the ghost story would be handed down from generation to generation and so kept alive as a result.

Anecdotes by their very nature become disseminated and distorted by time until eventually, they pass over into local folklore. It was hardly surprising, therefore, that when some locals were prompted by the authors on the subject of this legend, any positive replies were all very similar: *"Isn't it supposed to be a woman looking for her baby"* or some such similar statement was the normal response. With such a positive reaction, one can only deduce that the tale is alive and well and still occasionally doing the rounds.

Most local legends, however embellished by successive generations, generally have some basis in fact. Whatever people's perceptions are on this legend, very few have perceived the series of historical events that initiated it. When this sequence of events is brought together not only is a wonderful tale revealed but one can fully appreciate how the Rosevear island haunting came about.

When one visits Rosevear today, it is difficult to believe the events that happened there. However, the grand ball, the growing of vegetables and men experiencing supernatural agency as a group are all proven to be factual; substantiated by the various references above. With that in mind, it is not unreasonable to accept that a macabre discovery was also made on Rosevear. We now aim to add credence to this unsubstantiated part of the legend with facts that occurred before James Douglass was even born, as well by the presence of physical evidence remaining on Rosevear island from his time there.

Even if, like we the authors, you do not actually believe in the supernatural, the lighthouse builder's tale which follows is still an interesting saga that needs to be recorded. Certainly the story cannot be ignored, as it is directly related to the past lives of some rather fascinating eighteenth century people and the factual events that surrounded them.

Important note - Some of the following chapters contain passages that have been dramatised for entertainment value. These passages are written in a different font. These are, however, based on known facts discovered from our research. We have also used the names of the actual people with which the story is associated.

The lighthouse builder's tale which follows, is a fictional tale based on local legend. However, the fascinating factual events presented in the rest of the book will prove that the legend is actually based on fact.

To one grave they were committed
Scilly's earth on them was cast,
Cargill will no more delight us
these fleeting pleasures now are passed.
Robert Maybee

3. The Lighthouse Builder's Tale

Ruins of the blacksmith's workshop on Rosevear island (Circa 1900)
Viewed looking southwest
(Courtesy of the Gibson family of Scilly)

James Douglass, the joint Chief Engineer of the lighthouse building project, sat on the highest point of Rosevear island. He had actually grown to loathe the island but this promontory was his favourite place while there. He looked across to the Bishop Rock, his mind recalling the vast amount of work recently performed there. He then drew on a clay pipe sending billows of smoke spiralling into the fresh clean morning air and reflected on everything else that had happened to the men during their long stay among the Western Rocks. They had endured blistering heat; driving rain; howling gales; and seas so violent the spindrift had pelted them with stones and shells. On such occasions they would huddle together in their cottage and instead of listening to the noise of the pebbles on the roof outside, or boulders rumbling around in the surf, they would play music on their instruments.

Once in a while, during high spring tides, a huge sea would be driven in on a gale of wind and almost every wave would send heavy spray cascading down onto the roof and walls of their abode. Sometimes the sea even came flooding in through the small rickety wooden door. At such times they would move as much as they could above floor level and, fearing for their very lives, dare not step outside until the tide had receded away.

Even among a large workforce, with no female company around loneliness set in amongst the men. With all the down time caused by bad weather or rough seas, boredom was also inevitable. Fatigue would set in from the simple fact that living in such an environment was a stressful exercise in itself. Moments of melancholy also set in all too frequently as the men found themselves with plenty of time to think of their loved ones. Death and shipwrecks had also been encountered at first hand. In fact, on one particular occasion during the project, the men had set off to work as usual in their boat. The morning sun was high over St Agnes but there was still some thick fog hanging around Bishop Rock from the previous day. Hoping the fog would soon lift they entered it and steadily progressed on a compass bearing towards the construction site. Suddenly, flotsam and jetsam appeared in the water all around their boat. As they moved slowly forward through the disorientating and damp fog, the debris seemed to grow ever thicker. Eventually they found themselves having to avoid larger sections of floating wreckage and were even forced to use their oars over the bows of the boat to push individual pieces aside.

The work on the lighthouse had thus far progressed little further than the construction of a cofferdam. The men landed on the Bishop Rock and climbed up the ladder that would take them over the dam's iron wall to descend inside to start work. As the first man reached the top of the wall he was immediately faced with a group of shipwreck survivors, all huddled together in the bottom up against the curving wall of the cofferdam. The poor souls were found wet through; extremely pale looking and shivering uncontrollably with hypothermia resulting from the exposure. From their damaged half-naked bodies, it was obvious to see what sort of horrors they had endured during the night; but these were the lucky ones. Other victims of the vessel *Belinda*, wrecked on the rock during that dark night, weren't so lucky. The workmen later witnessed many corpses floating by lifeless on the tide. All these bodies needed to be picked up and stored on Rosevear until the boat came to take them away. James had many other sad memories to recall but one, which innocently involved the growing of vegetables, he would really rather forget. The subject became so emotive between some of the men that most of them preferred not to speak of it among themselves whilst they continued to work on the island. Certainly it was not spoken of within earshot of the head blacksmith who was extremely sensitive to the subject. Fortunately for James, the feelings he harboured for his sweetheart Mary Tregarthen on St Mary's often diverted his attention. Nevertheless his thoughts all too often drifted back to the moment when all the trouble so innocently started.

Day after day, week after week and month after month the men had been toiling with large blocks of hard granite. Consequently, James Douglass subconsciously felt a growing need of something more delicate and organic to do with his spare time. Driven by a very basic and intermittent food supply, due to the supply boat often failing to materialise in bad weather, James decided to grow some fresh vegetables for the group. One Sunday morning he took some tools from one of the workshops and started testing the depth of earth around the cottage with a fork. Understandably, there was precious little in the way of earth. There was an overall covering of about a foot; deeper areas of earth were simply where it had accumulated in large fissures and crevices in the solid bedrock. He identified a suitable area of relatively deep soil and started clearing away the wild plants that grew over it. As he started to dig, little did he know that he was about to make a rather macabre discovery. He pressed his fork into the ground and

tilted back the handle. He then lifted a shrub and ran the earth encased roots through his fingers, separating them and letting the loosened earth fall back to the ground. *The soft texture of this soil feels so good after all that stonework* he thought to himself. As his fingers tickled earth away from the roots he noticed a few harder objects were also falling down around his feet. These objects did not appear to possess the density of stones or pebbles, so he bent down to pick one up and began to examine it. Bringing the object up to eye level he scrutinised it more closely. *Animal Bones,* he thought, *how odd to find these all the way out here in this desolate place.* He then returned back to the task in hand. Again and again he dug the earth but with similar results. With every forkful of earth lifted, bones were found entwined within every uprooted shrub. Undeterred, James carried on casting any bones aside onto what was becoming a small but steadily growing heap. The fork went in again and again until, to one side, he noticed a dome like shape parched white by the sun. Immediately James placed his fork to the ground by its side and pushed it in under the object. As a result of finding all the other bones, James was only too aware that he could well expose a skull at some point. After loosening, he lifted the object free of the ground. At first sight it became alarmingly evident that he was not disturbing the remains of dead animals as he initially thought; these were in fact the remains of long since deceased human beings. The moment James perceived the skull was human, he stopped work and went back to the cottage to seek guidance from his brother William. *"Will",* he said poking his head round the door with a worried look on his face, *"I've been clearing away an area of shrubs for my vegetables but I've unearthed something I think you should see."* The two men went to see what James was referring to. The other workmen, who had also become intrigued, followed after them.

Arriving back at the spot James started to explain the situation to his brother. *"I found the earth in this area to be the only place even remotely suitable for growing anything at all. The trouble is, as you can plainly see, it appears to be some kind of burial ground."*
"Well just cover it over again," said William' but James looked disappointedly back at his brother as he had hoped for a more positive response. *"Well,"* he said trying to seek William's approval, *"this is the only suitable place for my plot. D' you think maybe I could just move the bones to another place so that I can carry on."* Silence then fell for a brief moment as James waited for a quick and favourable response but when nothing was immediately forthcoming in reply, he tried to aid his cause by adding, *"I mean, it seems a shame to stop now, especially as I've disturbed so many of the remains already."* William was the only other senior man on the project, so there was no one else to turn to for advice and guidance. This, however, was a subject rather unusual to William as well, and a problem that needed to be given a little thought before answering. *"Hmmm,"* said William rubbing his chin, *"to be honest, I seem to recall that this same problem happened once before."*
"How do you mean?" asked James in amazement knowing this kind of thing doesn't happen every day.
"Well, it may only be a rumour but as I remember it, the chaps who built the original wooden buildings here that we used when building the first lighthouse under our father's guidance, also uncovered some human bones when they laid the foundations."
"Well how did they deal with the bones they found?" asked James hoping to do the same.
"I think they were under great pressure to get the job done, so simply moved them aside and covered them back over," answered William looking pensive while trying to remember the story.

"Then perhaps I should simply do likewise," said James.
Given the circumstances, it certainly seemed a quick and reasonable solution to William, who saw no harm in simply repeating history. *"I can't see why you shouldn't relocate those you've already disturbed,"* he said confidently.

Looking on was a small blond curly-haired stout Scillonian workman named Robert Maybee, who was standing next to Samuel Rowling the head blacksmith. Described as an insignificant man, Maybee was a common labourer who generally worked on farms and in the kelping industry. He was a sensitive soul and a popular accomplished local poet. Rowling, on the other hand, was a large man, almost completely bald and over sixty years of age. Regardless of being the oldest worker on the project, being a blacksmith had kept him strong, fit and healthy. Rowling was a master of his trade and had been brought in from the mainland especially for this job. He was a loner and, when not working on Rosevear, he had taken up residence on Tresco; preferring it to the relative hustle and bustle of St Mary's. Rowling was set in his ways; the stubborn sort who, once he'd got an idea into his head, nothing would shift it. Having spent most of his life working alone, Rowling was also a little on the sensitive side. This part to his character, however, tended to border on the paranoid. He was also God fearing with strong religious beliefs. Looking down at the bones Rowling not only found the scene sacriligious but also deeply disturbing; he was already muttering his displeasure to the labourer Maybee beside him, who appeared to be feeling sympathetic. As a result Maybee also grew steadily agitated by what was being suggested. Suddenly Rowling spoke; *"Oh, that's just a great idea Mr Douglass,"* he said sarcastically, *"let's just go ahead and dig 'em all up shall we?"*

"I don't see why that's such a problem," said William trying to retake command of the situation, *"after all, these remains have probably been moved once already, and for all we know, they could even be thousands of years old."* William felt just as bad about the situation as anyone else but having a mere tradesman question one of his decisions was a slap to his ego.
"Well I don't like it either," said Maybee gingerly but in a rather discontented manner, adding weight to the argument, *"it ain't right nor proper disturbing the dead like this Mr Douglass,"* he added. Silence then fell over the scene as the realities of the situation sank in with everyone present. Most suddenly found themselves thinking how they, or their families, might feel if someone disturbed the bones of one of their loved ones. William, on the other hand, was simply in shock. It was the first time he had ever been doubted by any of the men; and couldn't quite grasp that they were not questioning his authority, just this one decision. Breaking the silence, the blacksmith spoke again, *"You mark my words Mr Douglass,"* he warned sternly, *"this is bound to bring us naught but ill will."* William and James were both taken aback as Rowling's' words suddenly sparked further uncomfortable shuffles and mumblings from other members of the team. *"I do hear what you're saying Sam,"* said William directly to Rowling in agreement. He then tried to defuse the situation by adding, *"I don't like it much either but it's a bit late in the day now, James has probably already moved most of them aside."*
"I just thought they were animal bones," interjected James defending his actions and rather upset that he had caused such a problem. However, his explanation was like a flame igniting fuel under a much more heated debate that then ensued between everyone present. After a moment or two of argument William interrupted *"Look,"* he said loudly trying to keep the decorum

and then attempted to pacify the workforce by saying, *"why don't we give these poor souls as proper burial as we can in one single common grave. We can even mark the spot with a headstone. Surely that would be better than just leaving them where they are now."* Further mumblings of disgruntled men followed, to which James, in wanting to continue with his vegetable garden, added *"Williams's right, I'll bury them properly like he says. I'll even cut a special headstone, so that their new resting place can at least be recognised as being a grave in future. This would stop this kind of thing ever happening again. Surely that's got to be better than the situation these poor devils have suffered thus far."* James' plea was accompanied with a gesture towards the overgrown shrubs and disturbed area of ground. This seemed to appease a couple of the men, so he looked to these in particular, hoping to influence them to spur others into a more favourable response. If nothing else, these men gave James a kind of half-hearted consent and it immediately eased how he felt. At this Rowling walked away mumbling and grumbling with displeasure, and his departure inspired the others to do likewise. As the men turned their backs, William looked at James and rolled his eyes; he then sighed and mouthed the words *"carry on,"* to his brother. James, still feeling uncomfortable, waited a while before continuing.

Once James was alone again, he tentatively poked around in the earth in a half-hearted attempt at looking for more bones. But as time passed, and he became more comfortable with it, he started turning over the ground just as he had before. Small areas of bones being exposed in deeper crevices had already identified most of the graves and these areas he finished clearing first. When satisfied there were no more remains to be found, James then fetched a wheelbarrow and piled all the bones into it. He then wheeled them a short distance to the southwest of the cottage where he identified a suitable place to re-inter them. James then chose a headstone and, even if just to show to anyone finding it later that it had been fashioned by the hand of man, he gave it a basic dressing. He then dug a shallow pit in front of the stone and surrounded it with rocks. The bones were then laid to rest in the encompassing rocks where James covered them over with earth. He then placed more rocks on top of the earth to further conceal the remains. After inspecting his work he gathered the others together again and asked for silence as he intended to say a few words over the scene. The men huddled around the grave and James removed his hat before starting to speak. The men followed suit and settled down to listen. With difficulty in finding the right words James spoke. *"Almighty God,"* he said trying to pluck the words from deep within, *"we know not who these poor people were, nor how they came to be here in this desolate place, but it was your will. We pray that we may be forgiven for disturbing their bones. We commend them again to the ground and hope that in your merciful way you have found their souls a place in Heaven beside you."* Then James bowed his head and said *"Let us all pray."* A minute or two of silent contemplation was then followed by the Lord's prayer; initiated by James. Once the short service was over, Rowling then chirped up with exactly how he felt about the situation, *"This is all very well and good Mr Douglass but this is not consecrated ground, nor we qualified enough to make it so."* In almost silent acceptance all agreed that Rowling had a very valid point and one that neither James or William had given any thought to. *"True enough Sam,"* said William sticking up for his kin *"but then where the bones were originally situated was hardly likely to have been either."*

"Aye probably not," admitted Rowling as sarcastically as before

"but then who wouldn't now agree, that we wouldn't all be better off if the bones had remained undisturbed where they were, with us in ignorance of them."

"Aye," said Maybee loudly in agreement, making William ever more uncomfortable with his earlier decision, but he tried not to let it show as he attempted to appease everyone's sensibilities.

"Look," said William attempting to stay calm *"it's clear that none of us is completely at ease with the situation but what's done is done, so there's no use in us keep going over it."* Very disgruntled, Rowling then went to speak again. *"However....,"* he said but was immediately interrupted by William, who cut him off with further attempts at appeasement *"No Sam, maybe no one here is qualified, but we have done the best we can with a bad situation."* William had spoken loudly but again Rowling tried to speak his mind. *"Well I think....,"* he said but again William cut him off. *"A situation, I might add Sam, inadvertently brought upon us by my brother. But then who knows, perhaps it was God's will that James found the bones, so that we might rebury them properly as we have done; and as you often say, Sam, God does work in mysterious ways."* To this Rowling could think of no retort, and William glared at him hoping that was in fact the case; and the end of the matter. Rowling looked unimpressed. Under the circumstances, William knew it would only be a matter of time before superstition set in through weak-minded types like Rowling and Maybee, and, like an illness, start infecting others.

"It don't bode well is all I'll say on the matter," said Rowling, and he walked away confident in the fact that at least some of the other men seemed to agree with him. Stunned, William and James were left firmly rooted to the spot. It was inconceivable to either of them that any of the men, hand picked for the project by themselves, could even think of harbouring false notions as to

what may transpire as a result of relocating a few old bones.

Before long, James and William were left alone by the grave. *"Sorry Will,"* said James knowing he had inadvertently upset the delicate equilibrium between isolated men, and by so doing, created a potentially volatile situation.
"Its not your fault," replied William gesturing down at the newly constructed sepulchre, *"I personally think its time we all had a long deserved break from this God forsaken place, lest we all get cabin fever and end up like those poor souls."* He then sighed with frustration and ran one hand over his forehead in utter disbelief.
"Aye," said James in agreement with his younger brother *"it's been a long two years but, by our lady there's a lot left here to do yet."*

Williams' concerns towards possible cabin fever were extremely valid. Not only were the team physically cut off from the outside world, they had little to no communications with it either; at least until the small supply boat arrived, or the working steamer bringing materials came their way. Adding to the lack of regular contact with other human beings, they also had no power and only a limited supply of fresh food and clean water. They now found themselves to have been living in isolation on top of a burial ground and to make matters worse, James had now thoroughly disturbed the graves of that cemetery. It is almost unimaginable how they were going to feel after each and every sunset from then on. Under such circumstances, it was completely understandable that they then went on to have more than a few rather odd experiences.
The weeks following the incident passed relatively

uneventfully although comments about the affair sparked accusations along with the odd disagreement. Nevertheless, the work progressed on schedule and James's vegetable garden became part of the scenery. The sight of the fresh newly constructed grave, erected just a short distance from the front of the cottage, stood as a permanent reminder of the uncomfortable episode. To William and James it became a monument to their one and only failing during a grand and noble project. Apart from any hidden bad feeling about the grave, everything appeared just as it should. However, it wouldn't be long before individuals reported having some rather odd experiences. These experiences usually involved either heavy objects moving of their own accord, or the belief of hearing music from an unexplainable source. As a result the men, especially the blacksmith, would not be left alone on the island.

Maybee was assigned to accompany Rowling as his labourer every day to alleviate the problem. Unfortunately this had a detrimental effect, as Rowling filled Maybee's head with impending doom. He also put each and every unexplained incident down to James Douglass having disturbed the dead of the island. Having Maybee agreeing with Rowling did not make life on Rosevear easy and consequently this forced James and William to split them up. William also suggested that perhaps James should temporarily leave the project until things returned to normal. James agreed and took the opportunity to leave Scilly to pursue another engineering qualification. He would be away from the project to study for months at a time.

Maybee was relocated back on St Mary's where he was put to work on Rat Island. Here he spent the rest of the project helping in the initial dressing of the stones for the lighthouse. Maybee's replacement on Rosevear was someone less corruptible, so Rowling was left without anyone to gripe to.

When James finally retuned to the project, he found circumstances on Rosevear were still far from normal. Occurrences believed to be of a supernatural nature had increased but the men were reluctant to talk about them. As a result, relationships had become strained, forcing the men to keep their minds to the task in hand; and unlike construction workers the world over, there was very little in the way of frivolity. Everyone was keen to complete the lighthouse as soon as humanly possible.

Surely thou hast another lot'
There is some home for thee,
Where thou shalt rest, remembering not,
the moaning of the sea.
Unknown author

4. Leaving Rosevear

Relieved to finally be leaving Rosevear, the men gathered everything together and waited inside the cottage for their transportation to arrive. James, on the other hand, had elected to sit out in the sunshine and keep a lookout for the boat that would finally take them away from their long ordeal. Sat on the highest point of the island and overlooking the cottage, James played on his flute; his mind empty of past events and thinking only of seeing his new wife again soon. Eventually his thoughts returned back to the job at hand; and, squinting eyes against the sunlight, he looked off into the distance for the boat. His gaze moved towards the main islands six miles away to the east. His attention then turned towards the south where, amidst the sun glistening water, he perceived a vessel coming into view.

Silhouetted in the distance against the bright background, the vessel silently rounded the southernmost tip of St Agnes, the nearest inhabited island, then continued on a course, bearing in the general direction towards the Western Rocks.

Puffing a steady stream of smoke into the clean air and towing a large wooden punt astern, the St Mary's registered steam tug *Bishop,* with its crew of six, drew ever nearer to Rosevear. Master of the vessel is Trinity House Pilot Jim Hicks. Hicks, a thick set man with short dark hair and trimmed beard, was originally a ships carpenter by trade but had left Scilly as a youngster. Remaining dedicated to the sea, he then sailed all the oceans of the globe during his lifetime. On returning to the islands, however, he had undertaken the job of sailing to and from Rosevear and the Bishop Rock, keeping the lighthouse workmen steadily supplied. Piloting south of the islands and heading on a south-westerly course, the vessel stood clear of any danger. The steamer then altered course to the northwest to pass through a gap in the islands called the Neck of Gorregan. Here the *Bishop* moves into the danger zone, entering the infamous Western Rocks. Skilfully Hicks guides the vessel around Gorregan Island, avoiding many hidden rocks in his way, to finally come about onto a direct heading for Rosevear.

Out in the early morning daylight James stopped playing his flute; screwed up his already sun wrinkled face and squintied to gain a better view of the approaching vessel. Recognising, as expected, it to indeed be the men's transportation, James got to his feet and made his way back down to the small granite dwelling. Putting his head around the door he alerted his colleagues of the approaching vessel outside. *"Its coming, Will,"* he says to his brother, *"the boat is on its way."* William stepped through the low doorway and came outside. *"Very well,"* he said, lifting his hand to his eyes to shield them from the sun, while checking the sighting for himself. *"I s'pose we should get our gear down to the jetty,"* he added scratching his thick black beard and pulling on his woolly hat for the journey ahead.

Within moments the workmen started cutting a steady path between the buildings, relaying tools and belongings along a sturdy wooden walkway down to the waters edge in Rosevear Neck. Eventually a large mound of clothes and equipment was piled up at the end of the jetty. William Douglass then went to take one last look inside the cottage and adjoining workshops, making sure that nothing was being left behind. Satisfied that everything was present and correct, he made his way to join the others waiting down on the jetty. Soon enough the steamer came within ear shot of the workmen who could hear the regular beat of its iron heart coming across the water. Master Hicks heaved the vessel to, bringing the steamer to a stop just off the eastern rocky shoreline of the island. *"Away anchor!"* is then clearly heard shouted from the small oblong shaped wooden wheelhouse. The next moment one of the vessel's iron anchors is released from the bow to splash into the water below. The small punt is then drawn up towards the vessel's stern. Shortly after two men climb on board and put out towards Rosevear Neck where the workmen are awaiting pick up from the wooden jetty. On board the steamer Jim Hicks leaves the engine running and moves over to the side of the vessel. Here he lights his clay tobacco pipe and watches closely as the punt is loaded with men and their belongings. Knowing it will take more than just one trip to get everything and everyone safely aboard the vessel; he draws on

his pipe and estimates it to be at least three trips. As expected after the punt takes its third and final trip across from the jetty, William Douglass is the last man to step up aboard the steamer.
"Welcome aboard again, William," greets Master Hicks removing his pipe from his mouth, while holding his other hand out in greeting.
"Thank you, Jim," William replies, removing his hat in respect and shaking Jim's hand. *"Hopefully this is the last time,"* he adds. Jim then pats William on the shoulder whilst nodding in recognition.
"Off out on the beer tonight then, to celebrate a job well done?" he asks pointing at the distant lighthouse while referring to the long years William and his men had spent building it. *"Well to be honest,"* replies William, *"and don't take this the wrong way, but as much as the men and I like Scilly,"* he then paused mid sentence trying to choose his words tactfully, knowing there were at least four Scillonian men aboard the steamer, *"but we're a bit tired of small places and just want to get off home; today if there's a boat going."*
"Yes of course, I can fully understand that," said Jim *"it must have been little short of a prison sentence being out here year upon year."*
William screwed his face up at Jim's reply, not quite sure how to put his true feelings into words. Yes, it had been a tedious, lonely, even dangerous job at times, but William had something else to convey as to why some of them felt the need to get away from Scilly. *"Yes,"* he then said, *"there is of course all of that."* William then lowered the tone of his voice a little before elaborating. It was the first time any of them had spoken properly about their experiences and he felt the need to relieve himself of the tension but opted to do it quietly. *"But to be perfectly honest Jim,"* he replied speaking softly *"we're all feeling a bit tense."*
"Why what's happened?" asked Jim, in an inquisitive tone.

"Well, and don't laugh at this, Jim, and you can even call it cabin fever if you want, but we were a bit spooked by something on that tiny island." Jim heard William's words only too clearly but had something more pressing to attend to first before asking what William meant by them. *"Secure the punt aft. Up anchor and prepare to get underway,"* shouted Jim to his crewmen on deck before turning back to the conversation. *"Go on, Will,"* he asked with intrigue.

"Well, in certain conditions, we're sure we could hear a woman humming what sounded like a lullaby, and Jim, you know that apart from the party we threw that one night, we've had no women out there with us." William then stopped and looked directly at Jim expecting ridicule or something like it in return, but Jim remained silent and just looked, with a blank expression on his face, directly back at William. *"Well I have actually heard through the island's bush telegraph that Bob Maybee had said something odd was going on out here, but to be perfectly honest I thought nothing of it."*

William's eye then twitched as a result of hearing that Robert Maybee had been telling the islanders Rowling's' version of events. He then drew even closer to Jim's ear and continued with what no one but he, and his men remaining on the island, knew. *"Well whatever's been said, that's not the whole story,"* replied William confidently *"I tell you now Jim, there's something up with that island; it sang to us."* William was now almost talking at a whisper and was about to elaborate further when Jim interrupted him, *"Singing?"* he queried in disbelief, *"you sure you weren't hearing seals wailing?"* he asked. William shook his head. *"Especially the newborn, they often do you know,"* offered Jim.

"No," said William indignantly, and then went on to press his point, *"I tell you Jim, this was a human singing voice."*

"Young gulls also whine a bit too sometimes," Jim added.
"God's truth Jim," interrupted William with a mild growing frustration at the skipper's snap explanations *"gulls and seals don't damned well sing lullabies do they?"*
"No, not even on Scilly," said Jim laughing in acknowledgement, but the seriousness on William's face, soon cut his amusement short. *"Listen Jim, most of the men had heard it individually at one time or another and all said the same thing. It was like a woman humming a baby a lullaby and, by our lady Jim, if one night we didn't all hear it together. Ask the others if you like."* Jim could see by William's countenance he was deadly serious and from what he knew of him as a person, William was not one to make up such a wild story.
"One night she woke us all up with her wailing, soft though it were, and at first we discussed it among us but no-one was brave enough to step outside the house to take a look. Eventually I said, we're all acting like children, and perhaps we ought to be searching the island together, just in case some poor devil's in trouble."
"Go on," said Jim.
"Well, with that we all went outside and searched among the rocks of the island together, calling out and that, and all the time we could hear this low singing coming and going on the wind. We heard it most on the western side of the island, where it seemed to be coming from just out to sea." Jim's face then changed, he was a man who liked to be taken seriously himself, so didn't like to be seen to be superstitious or believe in ghosts, ghouls, goblins and their like. As a result he chose his words carefully and in an attempt to bring William a modicum of comfort, he succinctly stated, *"It ain't the first time I've heard such a tale, Will, and I'm certain it wont be the last."* He then returned to his duties; *"Reverse course back to St Mary's boys; we'll not spare the horses, the workmen have*

another boat to catch."

"What do you mean?" asked William regaining the skipper's attention.

"Well I don't really believe in such things, but local fishermen have heard the lullaby to on occasion and always when working near this same Island," said Jim lifting his head to scratch the flesh beneath his unshaven chin.

"Thank God for that," replied William with a sigh of relief *"We all thought we were going mad, especially after my brother had dug up all those old human bones an' all."*

"What bones are these?" asked Jim inquisitively, realising the men obviously had some bizarre experience, with some kind of misgivings about the situation; there was obviously more to the tale than Jim had previously overheard from Maybee.

"Well during a down time James decided to try and grow a few vegetables but in creating a little clearing he unearthed a scattering of human remains just below the surface."

"Really?" interrupted Jim, *"how odd, do go on."*

"Well, realising he had uncovered an area of graves, we did the only thing we could, we placed all the bones in a common grave and gave them a Christian burial. We also marked the spot with a basic headstone and said a few words over it."

"So what's wrong with that?" asked Jim not realising William had sanctioned his brother to further dig up and remove all the remains against some of the other men's wishes.

"Well the trouble is," said William keeping that part of the tale to himself, *"as we had no pastor on the island to do the honours over the scene, this left one or two of the men feeling a tad uncomfortable about the whole thing. A little like we had only half done the job so to speak."*

"Mmmm, yes," said Jim thoughtfully, *"I can see how some might*

worry in such circumstances, although I am sure the good Lord will understand; after all, you did re-bury them." Jim was making an attempt at bringing a little comfort and so softening the event, but William clearly remained uneasy.

"Yes, yes, I'm sure he does," replied William in a kind of uncertain acceptance, his memory then recounting other strange incidents some of which involved heavy objects appearing to have been moved without the aid of any human intervention. William wasn't quite ready to relay every last detail of the saga as it all seemed a bit on the ridiculous side. He hadn't witnessed many of the events himself but remembers well how the men occasionally needed to be coaxed back to work. He was also unsure as to whether some of the events hadn't just simply been purposely manufactured by someone to deliberately make him feel uneasy. A short interlude then ensued as both men gave thought to the strange subject of conversation. William, for his part, could think only of more questions, and like the rest of his men, he had been wondering if the remains and the strange noises he had heard were in some way related. After choosing which question to ask next he finally spoke again. *"So, Jim, what do you think is behind all this then?"* Jim now felt forced into a corner, he didn't want to perpetuate what he indeed saw as a possible case of cabin fever, or nonsense of the weak-minded, and was certain there was some perfectly reasonable explanation for the odd noises often heard around Rosevear island. William, however, was obviously a man in need of an explanation and Jim could see he was awaiting a reply. *"Ann Cargill,"* said Jim with a modicum of impatience and hoping not to have to elaborate much further, *"that's who some will say does all the singing."* This news only intrigued William all the more. *"Ann Cargill?,* he asked inquisitively *"who was she then?"* Jim did not reply immediately but instead appeared to stare out into the

beyond for some kind of divine guidance. After a few seconds had passed he finally spoke, but it was almost like he was quoting poetry or something of that kind. *"The maternal instinct had not yet yielded even unto death itself,"* he said. Understandably William did not quite comprehend Jim's completely nonsensical statement. *"What's that supposed to mean?"* he felt compelled to ask in almost total bewilderment. *"Oh nothing,"* said Jim, *"Just something someone recalled in their memoirs during the aftermath of a shipwreck hereabouts."* Like many Scillonian men Jim had long since been interested in local shipwrecks and one in particular was still occasionally brought back to mind. Furthermore, this tale of a ghostly voice singing over Rosevear island brought the story of the wreck flooding back. For a brief moment, Jim, in thinking too deeply about the subject of conversation, almost forgot to do his job. Only the sight of the crew looking blankly at him for guidance brought him back to reality. *"All secure,"* he barked falling neatly back into his part as master of the steamer. *"Aye,"* came a sarcastic reply from a crewman. Jim then stepped into the wheelhouse and shifted a control lever that clunked audibly as the vessel was put into reverse gear. He put the wheel hard over, and then pushed another lever that powered up the engine. Slowly the vessel started to move astern. Jim then dropped the revs away, spun the wheel the other way; clunked the gear into forward and pushed up the revs again. This manoeuvre gave the steamer a sharper turn to get the bows to face away from the island. William went over to the wheelhouse that barely had room for two men and awaited Jim's reply. Once the steamer was motoring on a steady course, Jim then attempted to explain his strange statement to William, *"Well, Will,"* he finally said in resignation, *"it's a good half an hour back to St Mary's. So to pass the time I'll tell you the story of a celebrated and beautiful actress and singer named Ann Cargill, and how she, with child in arms, came to be lost in the wreck of the Nancy packet on the shore of this tiny island."*

We established in the first two chapters that events in the tale above existed. After now perceiving the tale, it is clear that we have one or two to things to prove before we can move on. Firstly, we must establish that human remains were in fact on Rosevear for the workmen to find in the first place, and secondly, that those men made their macabre discovery.

On the first point, it is a fact that many bodies had been interred on Rosevear and this will be proven beyond all doubt in later chapters.

As for the second point, we must remember that many workmen continually toiled on that tiny place during the years 1847 to 1888, with the foundations of several buildings being laid. To perform this work, areas of the land had to be cleared and flattened off before hand. It is therefore reasonable to assume that remains must surely have been encountered at some juncture. Further to this, we will show in a later chapter how someone, who merely visited the island for just an hour or so, wrote about encountering human remains during their short time on Rosevear. It must also be remembered that our version of the tale was set during the building of the granite lighthouse when all the reports of supernatural agency had been reported; this seemed the natural thing to do. It is, however, perfectly possible that the discovery of human remains did in fact take place when the first iron lighthouse was built, and the land initially cleared to make way for the wooden buildings. Either way, a mass grave for any remains discovered was an inevitability.

The reluctance of anyone, including James Douglass, wanting to record, or even admit to disturbing the remains of the dead is perfectly understandable; and possibly just one of many reasons why no references regarding this point have surfaced thus far. If

James' brother William had written a diary of his life, as he had remained on the island throughout the entire project, perhaps then we may have found something more tangible in the way of relating paper evidence.

So whose remains were interred on Rosevear island is the next question to consider? Well, we have already mentioned in an earlier chapter that victims of three known shipwreck incidents were found cast ashore on that desolate place; these were from the wreck of the *Thames* in 1841; the wreck of the *Nickerie* in 1844; and the wreck of the *Nancy* packet in 1784. The first two incidents show that victims of these disasters made it ashore on Rosevear but there are no records of any burials having taken place. However, the *Nancy* packet disaster is a completely different story!

Dismal is the tale,
which I now unto you relate.
Hearts which are not cold to beauty,
must lament a fair one's fate.
Robert Maybee

SECTION (2)

1. Miss Brown

The young Ann Brown dressed for the part of Polly
Circa 1774.
(Courtesey of the Harry Ransom Centre Texas USA)

Ann Brown was born in 1760 to respectable London coal merchant Edward Brown and his wife and being the only child, her father lavished her with attention. Although described as rather petite, Ann was an extremely pretty girl; a charming child with long dark hair, pale skin, high cheekbones and dark brown eyes. She seemed a typical young girl with a very normal upbringing and like most girls she loved to dance and sing and live in a world of make believe. The thing that set Ann apart as different was that she exuded charisma and possessed a very natural theatrical talent. When Ann showed off to gain attention, as young girls often do, anyone casting an eye in her direction actually found they took notice of her actions. After observing Ann many would comment to her parents on her ability to entertain and, as a result, Ann's father grew increasingly aware of his daughter's flair for all things theatrical. Like many fathers Edward was very attentive and protective of his little princess; indulging her every whim and nurturing her God given gifts. Actively encouraging Ann, he pushed her talents in what he thought was the right direction; an action he would later come to regret.

It all seemed so innocent to Edward when Ann was a child but things would soon become very different indeed as she blossomed into womanhood. With her father's help, Ann was on stage and *treading the boards* by the tender age of eleven. In 1771 Ann made her debut at London's Covent Garden theatre, making an immediate impact in the singing part of Titania, in George Coleman's' *The Fairy Prince*. She was a great success. In fact, she acquitted herself so well that celebrated Georgian composer R.J.S. Stevens described her as follows: *"Miss Brown acted Titania. She was very pretty, had a good voice and an excellent ear".* Not only that, all her initial notices praised her beauty and quality of voice, which immediately led to further roles being offered. Her rise in the theatre from then on was meteoric, with Ann becoming a child star in a relatively short space of time.

Over the following four years she remained attached to Covent Garden. She played *Sally* in Coleman's *Man and Wife*; she sang in the *Bach-Abel* oratorio season; and played the role of *Clara* in Richard Brinsley Sheridan's, *The Duenna*. Inevitably though, it was all happening much too fast, especially for a girl still in the delicate stages of puberty. Ann may have been petite but her physical virtues were developing rather quickly. By the time Ann was fifteen she had blossomed into an attractive young woman. Ann's physical virtues were comparable with another famous contemporary beauty of the time, Lady Emma Hamilton. Both women were brunettes with smouldering good looks that exuded passion and lust. They were both easy on the eye, thin in the waist but otherwise fairly full figured. Ann's problem arose when her make up, costumes and stage roles projected her as being much older than her actual years. As such, she became a very desirable target to any cad or *"Jack the Lad"*. Flirtatious in the extreme, Ann had the ability to mesmerize an admirer but was as yet unaware of the powers she possessed. This placed Ann in a vulnerable position, as she had no experience in how to recognise or handle unscrupulous types of men who wanted only to gain her as a trophy. Through her own naivety, she found herself in compromising circumstances time and time again. Although it is quite probable that the young Ann Brown thrived on the excitement and attention that the wrong types of men so readily provided. Nevertheless, when much later Ann became independent both physically and financially and could choose whomever she wished as a suitor, she still could not seem to make the right choices. As a result she had a string of meaningless relationships and sordid affairs. It was a path that made her flippant and fickle in all future relationships with men. Moreover, Ann had probably been spoilt by her father from an early age and because everything else later in life, career, fame and money, all seem to have attended her far too readily, she became frivolous in almost every aspect of her life.

At first, life seemed almost perfect for Edward Brown; his business was flourishing and his beautiful daughter seemed rather special. Although he was initially blind to her antics, Ann's promiscuous behaviour soon became all too apparent. The two characters were nurturing very differing aims for Ann's future life and Edward soon found it a struggle to protect his offspring from the advances of her growing throngs of admirers. Nevertheless, Ann enjoyed all the attention being lavished upon her and naturally fought to further advance her newfound popularity.

Like any teenager placed in a similar position, Ann was heading into conflict with her parents and soon showed signs of becoming wayward. Consequently there were continuous disagreements, many of which were sparked by things such as: Ann staying out late; Ann not divulging where she had been or with whom. The fact that there was a continual stream of male callers on the door step of her family home, also caused strain in her relationship with her parents. These divergences led Ann to openly flaunt one of her shallow affairs right in front of her father. It was an action that would eventually result in a series of more serious struggles between father and daughter. At this point the conflict really amounted to little more than the usual everyday family struggle over parental authority. It was, however, a battle both parties were determined to win. Edward tried to keep his daughter under close guard but the more stifling his grasp on Ann's life, the more rebellious she became. Ann was only human after all, with all the wants, needs and desires of any young woman but these were the very feelings in her that Edward was desperately trying to suppress. The conflict between them became a daily occurrence, with the comfort of the attentive father figure gradually eroding away from Ann's life. Subconsciously, this no doubt left a terrible void that needed to be filled. The tension was mounting and the continual struggle was to drive her into the arms of a much older man.

Ann's popularity increased during a role as *Clara,* bringing her only greater demand from an adoring public. It was during this time that she succumbed to the advances of one of her more mature admirers; gunpowder manufacturer Miles Peter Andrews; her senior by eighteen years. Andrews was also an amateur playwright. An arrogant successful business man whose gunpowder production factory was described as "*extensive*". He was from a rich family with plenty of money to spend on enjoying himself. Although described by his friends as *"a man about town,"* not everyone thought well of Andrews. One in particular, a Mr Jonathan Taylor, was unimpressed by the way Andrews encouraged Ann's apparent disappearing moral virtues: *"Andrews wrote a play, but the drama was far beyond the reach of his powers. He first excited the public attention by having seduced Miss Brown from the stage, when she was rising rapidly into fame by the beauty of her person and her musical and theatrical talents. But the subsequent conduct of this lady strongly indicated that he had little reason to pride himself on the triumph of his gallantry, as it is by no means improbable that any other assailant, with an equal opportunity, would have been equally successful."* It is difficult to see just who was to become the victim in this wild passionate and short-lived relationship. Certainly Ann, for her part, was probably just going through normal teenage angst; inadvertently using Andrews as an excuse to break all ties with her father. Andrews, however, was married and probably just adding a large and rather famous notch to his bedpost. Regardless of his intentions, Ann eloped with Andrews and disregarded her commitment to appear that night as Clara in the Duenna at a Covent Garden Theatre. It was later reported that: *"she was kissing the fiction into fact elsewhere."*

When in December 1775 the lovers returned, Edward tracked her down to an aunt who was sympathetic to Ann's cause. He then forcibly removed his daughter away from Andrews and took her before the visually impaired local magistrate, Sir John Fielding, known at the time as the 'Blind Beak'. It was reported in the Morning Post on the 6th that Ann was: *"forced from the arms of her gallant, by the vigilance of her father and the interposition of Sir John Fielding".* Mediating between father and daughter, Fielding heard both sides of the story. He then turned to Andrews, who was also present at court, and questioning his feelings for Ann, asked if he loved her. Andrews replied; *"Love her! More than life!" – "Why don't you marry her?"* asked Fielding, *"Because I am married already."* The Magistrate was clearly unimpressed and immediately gave custody of Ann to her father. However, this situation did not last more than a week as she again eloped with Andrews and moved back in with the sympathetic aunt. Here the couple were allowed to regularly come together. Morning Post 15th December 1775: *"Yesterday the little Syrene of Covent Garden theatre made a second elopement eluding the vigilance of her father."* A month later on Wednesday the 5th January 1776 he: *"apprehended the little wanton truant at her aunt's in the city"* As ever the story made headline news in numerous publications, reporting that: *"Edward forcibly removed Ann from London carrying her away, kicking and screaming, in a coach".* Trapped inside the vehicle Ann bided her time. When little more than five miles had passed by she had hatched her plan of escape. Being an accomplished actress, she used her talents to dupe the inhabitants of a small village, through which they were passing, into setting her free by declaring that: *"the man* (i.e. her father) *was carrying her away by force, in order to ship her to America".* With the resulting help of the local villagers, the free-spirited girl eluded her father's protection once again, *"when she ran to town across the country"* and promptly returned to her aunt's house in Covent Garden and to her lover Mr Andrews. She then resumed the 1776 theatrical season business as usual.

After Ann absconded from his care, Edward bided his time and hatched another plan to take into custody his wayward daughter. This he intended to do with the help of his friend, a Mr G. Stacy. This event was also reported in the newspapers showing how Stacy '*way laid'* Ann at five o'clock as she made her way to the theatre alone and then pounced. Stacy: *"seized her and violently forced her away. The mob, however, who heard and pitied her distress rescued her, and threatened the principal and his assistant with very severe discipline for their inhumanity".* A more comical report of the incident was printed in another London journal: *"Friday night the coal merchant, whose daughter eloped from him some months since, attempted to seize her, as she stopped in a coach at the end of the play-house passage in Bow Street. The little Syrene was accompanied by her aunt, who made a great outcry, and told the populace Mr Brown was mad; the alarm presently reached the play-house, and the theatrical garrison sallied out in great numbers... to relieve the distressed damsel. The thieves in the Beggars Opera, armed with pistols, & c, made a most formidable appearance, and the crowd was so numerous, that for a considerable time the street was impassable. At length, however, the lady was handed into the play-house in triumph, and, notwithstanding her great agitation of spirits, performed the part of Polly greatly to the satisfaction of a very numerous and brilliant audience, who received her with repeated shouts of applause".* Even after such a traumatic experience outside the theatre, what was not reported was the fact that Ann still took to the stage but in what appeared to be a very distressed state of mind. Her anguish surfaced as she began her performance in the Beggar's Opera: *"she came upon the stage in the character of Polly, burst into a flood of tears, and fell into Mr Wilson's arms in a swoon. After she was taken off, Mr Hull came on, and acquainted the audience, that the young lady's illness arose from an alarm she had met with about an hour before".* After a short while to gather her thoughts, she went on with the show but it was reported in the same newspaper article as being: *"under great anxiety of mind."* Some might have said that it was all part of an act giving no thought to the fact that she was actually still rather young. Whether her trauma on stage was real or false only Ann knew.

Mr Stacy was criticised in the press for his involvement and he replied with a long-winded account of his side of the story. Letters then flew backwards and forwards in the press as one side blamed the other for all the commotion. Eventually the public at large also found it necessary to write in, and, from the benefit of anonymity, criticised the saga being reported. Morning Post 9th October 1776: *Mr Editor. The town ought not to be troubled with the domestic concerns of the players and their relations. One Mr G Stacey has written a very silly account of his own silly conduct respecting Miss Brown. I think you are to blame, in permitting such stuff to be intruded on the public, through the channel of your newspaper. If Mr Brown has a legal right to prevent his daughter from performing on the stage, he has a legal remedy to enforce it, and he certainly ought not use any other means to prevent her, whatsoever.* Signed, *One of the public.*

Regardless of all the scandal the public at large had fallen hopelessly in love with Ann's talents and charm. In upper class circles, however, actresses were seen as little more than prostitutes and the Browns' airing their dirty washing so publicly was becoming a very tiresome saga. Furthermore, the knowledge that Ann, at only sixteen years of age, was being bedded out of wedlock by a much older man, only fuelled their ill beleifs. Ann's male admirers, however, only viewed the starlet as being ever more approachable.

All the rumours and letters in the press caused such great consternation to Edward that he too appears to have grown weary of the conflict. The dishonour, humiliation and chastisement had worn him down. Consequently, by Christmas 1776 he finally gave up on his attempts to protect his troublesome offspring. John Kemble: *"She at length eloped from her father's house, and I knew well the man who triumphed in her seduction. Her maiden name was Brown, and her father was a respectable tradesman, who was made miserable by her indiscretion.*

Ann had been referred to in numerous reports as a *Syren;* pointing towards her having an ability to lure men to their own detriment. Certainly it is obvious by the public's help and reaction to the attempted abductions and her subsequent stage performances, that Ann did possess a kind of magnetic charm. Certainly, Ann was leaving a growing amount of broken hearts in her wake. Andrews was next in the firing line and 'Syren' was gradually becoming an extremely good description. It was also suggested that Ann was following tradition by deliberately obtaining a scandalous reputation. Without doubt she mimicked the behaviour of an earlier infamous actress, Lavina Fenton, who also played the part of Polly some fifty years before her. Certainly the lower classes loved all the controversy that surrounded Ann and she went on to rapturous applause as *Miranda* in *The Tempest.*

John Kemble gives insight into the fan base of Ann Brown: *"By a very early display of vocal and even comic talent, she had become an amazing favourite with the public. She increased in beauty as she advanced in her profession, and became an object of attraction to the dissolute".* On her advancement he also wrote: *"She was the original Clara in the Duenna; a very delightful singer, and one of the most captivating women of her time; but the head was not strong enough to regulate the conduct of the charmer, and she occasionally filled the page with scandal."*

Father and daughter were now far apart both physically and

mentally. If Ann could distance herself from her father, then what chance did other men stand at conducting any kind of meaningful relations with her? Only time would tell.

Ann Brown in The Tempest 1776
(Courtesy of the Shakespeare Birthplace Trust)

We saw the strong man, still and low,
a crushed reed thrown aside!
Yet by that rigid lip and brow,
Not without strife he died.
Unknown author

2. Mrs Cargill

Mrs Cargill (nee Brown) Circa 1780
(Courtesey of the Museo Thyssen-Bornemisza in Madrid)

By 1780 Ann was in her prime; she had lost all her puppy fat and her head and nose had grown ever so slightly longer giving her a much slimmer appearance. She had grown her hair down to the base of her spine but regularly adopted the wearing of braids. The conflict with her father had long since ended, resulting in the attentive affections of the most influential man in her life being completely cast aside.

Ann was now under contract and earning the princely sum of £10 per week for her performances but her private life was becoming as big a drama as anything she acted out on the stage. Ann was also growing more fickle and difficult; showing all the signs of developing into a real live 'Prima Donna'. Another of her newfound traits was a complete failure to commit to any thing or any one person. After her battles with her father, nothing now seemed permanent to Ann Brown whose whole life was rapidly becoming one big bumbling scandal. Andrews being married was the biggest scandal thus far; this, and he being much older than Ann were all factors in the demise of their lengthy, if turbulent, love affair. Although, as reported in the Morning Post, the catalyst was most likely that Ann had fallen for the advances of someone much younger than her current partner: "*We are told her new lover is a Mr R Cargill"* a tall suave, good-looking Irishman: *"The little Brunette of Covent Garden, eloped on Saturday morning with her new Adonis,"* the report added. Whereas on the 9th of August 1780 the Public Advertiser described Mr Cargill in slightly greater detail: *"The public have been imposed upon in the story concerning Mr Cargill, who married Miss Brown of Covent Garden, being an Irish fortune hunter. The following may be depended on: Mr Cargill is a young Gentleman of family in the island of Jamaica, and not yet 21 years of age. He was, about 4 years ago at Eton School; from thence he went to Edinburgh, where he studied at that University between two and three seasons. About six months ago he became acquainted with Miss Brown, and a mutual affection-taking place they were determined to seal that affection by marriage.*

Cargill had informed Ann that he was the son of a wealthy diamond merchant, a circumstance he bandied around in public like a title. Son of a wealthy diamond merchant certainly sounded far more enticing and exiting to Ann than mistress or hussy of a gunpowder manufacturer. In a dramatic show of flippancy she not only broke off her relationship with Miles Peter Andrews, she also disregarded her contract and future commitments to the manager of the Bow Street theatre and promptly eloped to Edinburgh with Mr Cargill. The newspapers reported her every move, one even commented on her virtues by stating that she was: "*susceptible to the softer sensations of love, in which she is said to participate with a most nice and genuine gusto*" In secret, Ann Brown married Robert Cargill in Scotland in haste. Although this was probably because she was carrying his child. It was a big mistake. Although trying to keep their wedding a secret, the event was still reported in the Public Advertiser, where the couple were said to have: *"Married in Edinburgh, where they remained upwards of a week, Mr Cargill being universally acquainted there, although the name and profession of his new married Lady were kept a secret."* The bubble finally burst when Ann found out that her new husband was broke and actually evading creditors. John Kemble describes the situation: *"At length, tired even of disorder, she married; but her choice was, as might be expected, little advantage to her"* As a result the couple split and returned to London. Ann moved back in with her aunt and was tempted back to the stage with a contract for the winter season. However, her physical condition was becoming all too obvious as reported in the Gazetteer on the 19th August 1780: *"Mrs Crawford and Mrs Cargill are engaged at the Drury Lane Theatre for the Winter season: the latter not upon the most certain terms, as an expected pregnancy may render the late Mrs Brown of very little service to the managers."* It is not clear whether the child lived or died and as no records thus far found make any reference to her, or her aunt, bringing up the child, or the infant appearing in any later reports of Ann's movements; we can only assume that the child did not survive.

Ann had become the Marilyn Monroe of her day; a popular celebrity whose every word and movement was put into print. Her attempts at keeping her true circumstances secret all failed. Even the façade of still being happily married did not keep the newspapers away from the inevitable truth.

Regardless of the trials and tribulations in her private life, in 1781 Ann was reported as being enormously popular as *Macheath* in a cross-gendered production of *The Beggar's Opera*. Nevertheless, in another demonstration of extreme levity she broke off all commitments to the production half way through the theatrical season. Dressed in a soldier's uniform, she ran off to Bath for the summer disguised as a man. Once again she had eloped with a male companion. Many early newspaper reports stated it was with her husband, but it was later revealed to be George Coleman; the theatre manager's son. No doubt the jolly jape had Ann giggling all the way to Bath in the coach; putting on a deep voice to anyone she met along the way. The incident was best recorded in a passage from the Authentic Memoirs of the Life of Ann Wells: *"this enchanting siren* (Ann Cargill) *eloping with a near relative of the Manager, at a time when her name was announced to perform Macheath the ensuing evening, threw the little Manager into real distress; in the height of which he applied to Mrs Wells to perform the character; which she immediately complied with, and absolutely studied the character in two days. But now another obstacle arose to perplex this Manager. Mrs Cargill had gone off in Macheaths cloths. Mrs Wells was therefore obliged to beg the loan of a coat from one, and a waistcoat and breeches of another!"*

The Public Advertiser caught on to the true identity of the man with whom Ann had eloped by stating that*: "Mr Cargill has experienced some distresses, from which however, his wife's present engagement with Mr Coleman has luckily relieved him."*

The relationship Ann had with Mr Coleman (junior) was short-lived. The event caused him untold problems with his family and consequently problems with his job at his father's theatre.

Once Ann was bored with Coleman, he was left to repair the damage. The influential effect the girl had on men with whom she came into contact, was again best described by John Kemble, whose comment was probably meant in a more general way. Nevertheless his advice fits rather well with the saga surrounding Mr Coleman junior: "*It may, perhaps, be proper to exhibit a fuller account of her conduct, and her fate, for the chance of recalling others to a just sense of their danger."*

Mr Coleman (senior) was understandably upset and his anger may have manifested itself in a lighthearted description of Ann the eloper. Mysteriously overnight, posters entitled the *"Advertisement extraordinary"* appeared in the press and on walls and lamp-posts around London's Covent Garden theatre district: *"Deserted, on Tuesday last, from his majesty's corps in the Haymarket, Polly Macheath, Captain of the Beggar Company of Robbers. He took with him his regimentals, and a thread purse, containing twenty-seven tin shillings, and nine leaden six pences, belonging to the property man. He is five feet two inches high, of beautiful red and white complexion, when painted; is inclined to be fat, and has large breasts, that pert like those of a Woman; his legs are well shaped but of the feminine make, and his knees incline inwards. He is rather prominent behind, and walks with short steps. Whoever apprehends this deserter, and lodges him in any of the company's strolling prisons, shall receive twenty shillings stage money, over and above the reward for taking up deserters. He is supposed to have gone to Bath, disguised in Women's apparel."*

Signed
by order
Hamlet, King of shrews.

Ann did not return to the stage until the following autumn and that was in a theatre nearby and in another production. Having switched theatres the original manager, Mr Coleman (senior), naturally tried to sue Ann and her husband for breach of contract. A worried Ann Cargill attended court on the 29th November 1781 where her case was heard. The council for the defendant declared: *he would put an end to the matter at once, by setting up as a defence the minority of the defendants at the time of entering into the engagement."* There is no doubt that Ann put on a successfully contrite performance for the Judge, who did in fact rule that her contract with Mr Coleman was unenforceable in law by reason of Ann and her husband being under the age of twenty one when they signed it. The law is the law, nevertheless, the little problematic temptress should have been made accountable for her actions and made to pay for any damage caused. She should certainly have been made to pay some kind of recompense for financial losses sustained by Mr Coleman. Perhaps the Judge was a fan.

Ann Cargill's consistently wonderful performances during that winter, aided by continuous scandal, placed the now seemingly invincible young woman at the summit of her fame; but not without cost. Her rise had been to the detriment of her father; Miles Peter Andrews; her husband; George Coleman Junior; and probably countless others. However, sat in the audience of one of her performances, after she had again returned to London, was her next challenge, Captain John Haldane.

(Courtesey of the Harry Ransom Centre Texas USA)

This fair one she from England sailed,
Bound to India's golden shore.
From friends, relations then she parted,
but little thought to meet no more.
Robert Maybee

3. Child of Misfortune

Bookplate of the Haldane family Coat of Arms

John Haldane was born illegitimate in 1748 and raised by an aristocratic family; the Haldanes of Gleneagles, Scotland. Since his mother and father never married, John would never actually carry the title *"of Gleneagles."* Although the family coat of arms bears the word *"suffer"*, referring to tolerance, some of the family did seem to endure in the other sense of the word. His father died when John was quite young leaving his grandfather to raise him. As an adult, John was a full six feet tall with dark hair and a pale complexion. Like many who had taken to a life at sea, John had joined the merchant fleet at an early age. With the help and influence of the Haldane family, he worked his way up within the English East India Company. Confident and forthright John made Midshipman in his teens, learning his trade on many Company ships. He finally attained the rank of Captain in 1779 and was given command of the 770 ton, three deck ship *Mountstuart* of 26 guns. Captain Haldane was probably known to many tars to come under his command as '*Captain Calamity*', a nickname earned after many unfortunate mishaps throughout his long career. His luck was so bad that he was described by friend and colleague William Hickey as: *"The child of misfortune, having been cast away when mate of an Indiaman, losing everything he possessed."* When one unfortunate circumstance was compounded by the next, the list of his mishaps resulted in the Historical Chronicle finally describing Captain John Haldane as: *"one of the most unfortunate officers ever employed in the company service; tho a brave and skilful seaman some ill fate always attended him, which seems to confirm the opinion of fatalists, that some men are born unfortunate."* It was a dubious accolade since the East India Company had by then been in existence for one hundred and eighty four years.

Whether or not one believes in ill fate, curses or bad luck, at least three ships were blighted while under John Haldane's command. First in line was the *Mountstuart*. During his very first voyage as Captain this ship was captured during an engagement with the combined fleets of France and Spain. The *Mountstuart*, while carrying military stores bound for the East Indies, to be used by the armies in India, was in a merchant fleet sailing under the protection of the Royal Navy. The merchant ships and their escorts were no match for the vastly superior force they were suddenly pitched against. Consequently, the escorting naval ships quickly evaded capture leaving the merchantmen to fend for themselves. After a short engagement John was taken prisoner and his ship was taken as a prize and incorporated into the enemy fleet. John then shared a prison cell in Cadiz with his crew. Eventually, as was the custom of the time, John was released in an exchange of prisoners of rank and he probably returned to Scotland to recuperate. Soon after he was summoned to East India Company offices in London, where at an inquiry into the incident he was acquitted of all blame for the loss of his ship. Even so, Haldane's ill luck carried over to his next command the newly built 790 ton *Fairford* of thirty guns; a ship that was soon to be called *the "disastrous Fairford."*

Whilst in London, John paid a visit to the tailor's where he was fitted out with a brand new company uniform. Wearing it for the first time he was taken to the theatre to see a show starring the infamous starlet Ann Cargill. John sat in the audience in his bright new dazzling uniform, mesmerized by the beautiful creature on stage. After the performance John was invited back behind the scenes along with others to meet the cast. Ann moved slowly along the line of admirers, eventually stopping at the dashing Captain after having been taken in by his height, good looks and attire. John almost stood to attention when the petite girl looked up at him and flashing her eyes asked *"And you are?"* Obviously flustered, John tried to remain composed as he mumbled somewhat feebly *"Captain John Haldane Ma'am."* Seeing this imposing figure suddenly crumble into a more uncomfortable manner, Ann toyed with him a little. She stepped back and looked John up and down inspecting him like a soldier on parade. She then moved around to his side running a finger over his shoulder epaulet. She further amused herself by giggling as she disappeared out of his sight behind him. Even though a little gaunt and pale from his recent ordeal, John was still a very imposing and handsome figure of a man. His coat of dark blue had lapels of a lighter tone, fringed with the same golden embroidery as his epaulets. Golden buttons with a lion and crown motif adorned the coat's front and large turned over cuffs. In contrast, under this he wore a waistcoat of pure white with breeches to match. Looking down at his feet, Ann could almost see her reflection in his extremely shiny black shoes. *"Ooh, you are stuffy Captain Haldane,"* she teased emerging from his other

side, *"but then I suppose you military types often are."*
"I am in fact in the employ of the East India Company Ma'am, the commander of a ship in a merchant fleet, at your service," John corrected, attempting to put this playful girl in her place. *"Indeed you are,"* she again teased petulantly. Looking every inch the gentlemen, John lifted his right hand and offered it to Ann in greeting. His left hand, which clasped the cocked hat held loosely under his arm, never moved a muscle. John's demeanour did indeed make him appear rather stiff, proud and unapproachable but his countenance told Ann a very different story.

Like every other man before him, the flirtatious girl could see the attraction in John's eyes and she continued to beguile him with her charm. She took his hand, flashed her brown eyes and curtseyed as if in the company of royalty. She then turned and flicked her long dark hair across his face and dismissed him as she moved onto the next admirer. In that first brief encounter Ann had seen her every advance involuntarily returned. She thought John seemed perfect but did not show it as she moved along the line greeting one person after another. John stood in line unsure what had just occurred, and, perceiving this, Ann continued to toy with him. She then acted as though she had already forgotten of his very existence but deliberately kept catching his eye. In this manner she continued to tease as she pretended to enjoy making pleasant conversation with all the other men in the line up. By the time Ann had reached the end of what seemed an inexhaustible line of tiresome admirers, John was already turning to leave and he moved slowly towards the exit door. *"Are you always so rude Mr Haldane?"* Ann said loudly back down the line to John whose back was now turned towards her. *"Do you always leave without saying goodbye?"* Stunned, John turned back around and

regardless of his total bewilderment, apologised. *"Please forgive me Ma'am, but I've not been myself lately."* He then moved to step back into line. Ann sauntered back along the line and on reaching John again she said *"I'll forgive you only if you entertain me all day tomorrow, when you can tell me what troubles you so much as to make you want to leave my company."* John bowed his head in acceptance, *"It will be my pleasure Ma'am,"* he replied.
"You may call on me here at eleven after my morning rehearsal and please call me by my name, Ma'am sounds far too stuffy," insisted Ann. She then dismissed John for the second time with a flick of a hand. She then turned her back and walked away from him.

Over the ensuing days of courtship Ann soon learned the pedigree of the Haldane family. John on the other hand became fully aware of Ann's rather dubious reputation. However, with a flash of her white smile, a swish of her long flowing hair and a deliberately exposed ankle, it was as if Ann's questionable background had never existed.

The couple were seen out together all over London and meeting regularly their affair blossomed. They had only been seeing each other a short time but it didn't stop Ann asking John to take her to Scotland to present her to his family. John declined, however, as he had an important announcement to make. *"The reason I am currently delayed in London,"* he said putting an end to her many requests, *"is because of my imminent departure to India."* Ann, as she now had a tendency to do, offered to give up all commitments personal and professional to follow her knight in shining armour. *"Oh John, please won't you take me with you?"* she pleaded.
"How can I my dear?" he replied, *"You have a career and an adoring*

public. Not to mention…," he stalled, cutting his sentence short, not wanting to upset her.

"Not to mention what?" she asked indignantly. John lowered his voice to a whisper, then finishing his sentence added *"A husband; you're married to another, remember."* When Ann had made her mind up that she wanted something, as her past had shown, she wasn't averse to pulling out all the stops to manipulate the situation to her favour. Without thinking about the implications, she answered with a statement that shook John down to the ends of his shiny new shoes. *"I'm also pregnant, my dear."* she said sarcastically.

As John digested the surprising news Ann joined him aboard the *Fairford* and together they eloped to India. The departing scene was probably very dramatic, a manufactured and very public event that was reported in numerous places, including the memoirs of Haldane's friend William Hickey: *"Captain Haldane had taken in the Fairford the famous Mrs Cargill who was greatly attached to him, so much so as to relinquish the stage on which she attained much celebrity to follow his fortune."*

Only time would tell if this love affair was to be short lived, but what no one else knew was that Ann had indeed, for the second time in her turbulent life, fallen pregnant. The resulting child, a boy, was to be illegitimate like its father. The press later saw the pregnancy as probably the reason behind Ann's sudden and rather theatrical exit from England.

The first voyage of the *Fairford* proved to be an ill famed affair. Right from the start the records show it to have been fraught with problems. Anthony Fuller: *The ship was a disaster as it left Portsmouth on 11th September 1782."* Not only did the *Fairford* suffer generally in poor performance of design, which became very evident when the ship exited the harbour, but also in other unrelated ways. The crew must certainly have feared the *Fairford* to be heavily jinxed. Not only was it commanded by the calamitous, *'child of misfortune',* Captain Haldane, but the presence of such an infamous woman on board may not have gone down well with some of the crew either. When it became clear to the men that Ann was in an unlawful relationship with their unfortunate Commander, the fact only added to any superstitious tension. This tension was compounded with Ann regularly being described in newspapers as a *Syren; a Nymph with a voice sweet enough to lure sailors to their destruction.* Sullen murmurs of discontent must have swept the crew, convincing them the voyage was cursed. Certainly, in this regard, history would show the disastrous *Fairford* would not have long to wait to meet with a rather untimely, if spectacular, end.

With spreading canvas in the Ocean,
Swift the vessel sailed along.
Safe conveyed to the Indies,
The queen of beauty dance and song.
Robert Maybee

4. *"Eastward Ho!"*

This is how the Fairford would have looked burning in Bombay Harbour

On route to Bombay the couple would have undoubtedly spent every available moment together in Haldane's Great Cabin and out on deck. No doubt Ann would occasionally have sung and given free acting performances for the crew. As time passed Ann's pregnancy announced itself to the couple naturally. To disguise this fact from the crew, Ann took to wearing clothes that best disguised her predicament. Nevertheless, with such a long journey ahead the disguise would not last forever and Ann would soon have to accept that another great scandal was inevitable and looming just over the horizon.

After a long and difficult journey around the Cape of Good Hope, the ill-fated *Fairford* arrived in Bombay after several long months at sea. While in the harbour the ship was to remain the couple's home as John had to complete the ship's business. Unfortunately, as the ship was being unloaded a fire took hold below decks. It seems that mere carelessness was the most likely cause, although at this time there was turmoil among the natives against the British presence; especially when foreign visitors, of all trading nations, often treated the locals with utter contempt. This inevitably resulted in attacks on European property including shipping. The East India Company records only state that the fire was *unavoidable* Whatever the reason, within a matter of minutes the flames grew totally out of control forcing everyone aboard topside. With thick choking smoke now filling the vessel, Haldane gave the order to abandon ship. By the time the ships boats were full and ready to take the first of the people ashore, the ship became engulfed in flames; with heat so fierce that it forced those waiting to be taken off, to jump into the water to get away. It is not known if anyone was harmed but many, including Haldane, lost everything they owned in the disaster. The only thing of value the couple saved from the fire was Ann's personal jewellery. William Hickey wrote that his friend John Haldane: *"got command of the Fairford a noble vessel of the company's which upon her first voyage was destroyed by fire in the harbour of Bombay."*

Clinging to the sides of small boats that came to their assistance, the crewmen were conveyed to shore. Reunited at the quayside, John aided Ann ashore amidst the dramatic backdrop of the burning armed merchantman. With masts and rigging now ablaze, the harbour was filled with smoke and orange flames that licked at a darkening sky. Everyone would have ducked involuntarily when the powder magazine suddenly exploded, sending rockets of debris spinning high into the air. The shock wave from the blast swept across Bombay Harbour shattering windows in the buildings nearby. Any boats close enough to be affected by the blast either scurried away from the danger zone or were pelted by falling debris as it came splashing down into the water all around them.

Re-emerging from behind their hiding places, stunned people around the dock side would have seen, through the devastation, that there was no hope of saving the *Fairford.* When the fire reached the waterline, what remained of the hull sank to the bottom of the harbour. When there was nothing more left to see, Ann and

John were offered temporary residence by the local Governor, Mr Hornby, at his home in Bombay Castle. Many ex-patriot families who lived nearby no doubt had many questions to ask of the couple. Certainly the women, on seeing Ann's bulging stomach, would have been asking how far gone she was.To which her ill-thought out but truthful answer would probably have been *"Roughly four months." "Apart from the fire, did you have a good trip?"* was also undoubtedly asked. Immediately followed by *"when did you leave England?"* With Ann's answer also being along the lines of *"four months"* it didn't take a mathematician to work out that the baby was likely to have been conceived on the journey, if not immediately preceding it. Therefore it was highly unlikely that the child was connected with Ann's lawful husband. This news inevitably set chins wagging furiously among the British. On the face of it the couple were well-received by many, especially anyone aware of Ann's talents. However, this did not stop this latest scandal, surrounding the legitimacy of her impending child, from sweeping across the Bombay Presidency.

In the upper echelons of the British quarter of the city, Governor Hornby not only housed and befriended the couple he was sympathetic and helpful in other ways. Inevitably, however, not everyone would be as supportive or enamoured by Ann's presence in India. Indeed, some of the upper classes did not take kindly to someone so infamous, with such questionable morals, invading their space. Undoubtedly she could not have arrived in India under more scandalous or dramatic circumstances. Ann had stepped ashore from a burning ship carrying the illegitimate child of the Captain while eloping from her lawful husband whom she left in England. Ill-feeling towards all these circumstances were succinctly stated by William Pitt (the Younger), the Prime Minister who was then actively trying to re-establish the good name of the East India Company in the East. Certainly Ann Cargill was not the kind of person that was going to help Mr Pitt's cause. Pitt was outraged that: *"an actress should be defiling the pure shores of India".* In fact he ordered Ann's return to England but news of it would not reach India by even the fastest mail packet for at least three months.

Haldane was not without friends and fared somewhat better than his partner. Not only had the local Governor taken pity on John's situation, he helped him to get back on his feet financially. William Hickey again records the events surrounding his friend's fortunes: *"Mr Hornby, the Governor at the time, feeling for the heavy loss Captain Haldane then sustained, with the humane intention of assisting him lending him a considerable sum of money to purchase an investment".* Whatever the outcome of the Governor's attempts to help John, Ann's theatrical talents were to prove a veritable goldmine to the couple. Her earning ability in India was little short of remarkable when she again took to the stage: "*building a cast herself from whomever she could find."* In little over a year she was reported to have amassed a personal fortune. The couple's initial period in the East was a time spent in need of each other and the charity of others. John had the friends and contacts that allowed the couple to get on better in society as a whole. Whereas Ann's eventual return to the stage gave the couple financial stability until John got back onto his feet.

The fact that Ann went back to work almost immediately after giving birth did not detract from her initial performances. It was, however, detrimental to the couple as they strived to become a family unit. Even so, the child brought love into their lives and some kind of stability. Motherhood was to give Ann something she had long craved since her own childhood; a sense of place and belonging. She doted upon the child as much as John now doted upon her. If John could have married Ann, he would have done. However, all in the garden was not rosy.

Ann Cargill performing in the Duenna
(Courtesey of the Harry Ramson Centre Texas USA)

Golden treasure there she gained,
Numerous charms then drew a throng.
Hearts were conquered by her beauty,
Ears delighted with her song.
Robert Maybee

5. Mr L

Ann Cargill circa 1783
(Courtesy of the Pelham Gallery)

In India the public loved Ann. She continued to perform many of the operatic parts for which she was famous and to tremendous applause. Outwardly, Ann and John appeared to be a happy couple but behind the scenes the Prime Minister of England was putting pressure upon John's employers, the East India Company representatives in Bombay, to get the pair to return to England. Ann was distraught. She could see her acting career blossoming in India. It was hard work though, as she was forced to production manage all the shows herself. This did, however, bring in a lot more money than she had ever earned before.

The East India Company representatives were making it abundantly clear to John that he was to leave India and to take *"that woman"* with him. Although far from leaving the country, Ann was planning to take her shows on a tour of India's other major cities. Inevitably, with a child to consider, this drove wedges between the couple as

Ann fought against John and the East India Company for control over her future. This conflict of interests eventually forced Ann into the arms of yet another man, with whom she contrived her fifth elopement in eight years. The man she planned to elope with was an unnamed Company Writer, referred to in the records simply as: *Mr L.* A writer was a high position within the structure of the East India Company organisation. As a consequence, under the request of the Company, the identity of Mr L was covered up. His name remains a secret to this day. (The East India Company did, however, have a Committee of Secrecy which kept many files and a more thorough search into these could yet yield his name. These files will, however, need to be decoded)

With John and Ann's relationship being placed under a terrible strain, the situation was brought to a head when the couple were invited to a large dinner party at the home of Captain John Dempster; another East India Company Commander. Like all mothers, Ann could not bear to be out of sight of her child but with an ulterior motive in mind she attended the gathering at the Dempster household at John's side. Ann took the baby along with her and used the boy as a covering excuse, allowing her to run into the arms of yet another man:

At the Dempster Estate, the butler announced their arrival in the entrance hall. *"Captain Haldane; Mrs Cargill and son,"* his voice boomed loudly, bringing immediate attention from other guests, whose turning heads made them both feel uncomfortable. The hostess of the household had previously arranged for Ann to have an attendant look after the baby. A large Indian servant, wearing native headgear, approached Ann and showed her to an upstairs room; here a female servant girl was waiting by a cot to attend the baby. John understood why Ann brought the child along instead of leaving him at home with a babysitter, but what he didn't know, was that during the coming evening, Ann was going

to use the child's presence, as an excuse to help her slip away into the night with the enigmatic Mr L.

In the dining room sixteen couples, all attended by servants, were seated around a very large teakwood dining table. Most of the guests were East India Company Officers and Marines with their wives and spouses. Inevitably, John and Ann's relationship was all too often the topic of conversation. Occasionally a guest would pass the odd spiteful comment, but Ann had faced many holier than thou attitudes at upper class social gatherings like these. Even so, the evening progressed as expected with the noses of the small minded reaching skywards towards someone so common, base and, to their annoyance, popular with the masses. More worldly open-minded guests attempted to patch any damage by perhaps deliberately behaving a little over-friendly. Nevertheless, both types of human behaviour made Ann feel uncomfortable.
"I hate these parties," said Ann angrily to John, but out of earshot of the other guests, *"they're always so damned stuffy."*
"Well let's just try to be ourselves then perhaps we may even enjoy it," replied John realising he was in for another difficult evening. Ann couldn't possibly be herself, as that meant saying out loud exactly how she felt; she bit her tongue and put on a pleasant front. Luckily things eased a little as the couple were seated directly next to the very sympathetic Governor Hornby and his wife. As a result, the couple were at least able to relax just a little. Unfortunately Ann seemed to remain on edge and kept looking at the large clock at the other end of the room.

After the first course John watched as Ann left the table to go and check on their son. John wasn't a jealous man by any means but with Ann's well- publicised chequered past, he naturally harboured some suspicions towards her fidelity. As a result he looked at his pocket watch and timed her absence. Six minutes had passed before she returned to her seat. Halfway through the main course a similar thing happened, with John taking a passing interest that the event this time took just over seven minutes. Then, just as desert was about to be served, Ann slipped away for a third time. John thought little of this and carried on in general conversation with the other guests. After a while Ann's continued absence had John glancing towards the door every time someone entered the room. He glanced at his watch but this time he had not noted the time Ann had left his side. For some reason John's instinct was telling him he should be concerned but all he thought to do was to continually consult his pocket watch. *Perhaps the boy was a little unsettled among the strange surroundings,* he thought. Eventually he felt compelled to call a servant over to attend him and the closest was the tall proud Indian. *"What can I get you Sir?"* the servant asked in extremely good English for a native of the country *"Could you err......."* said John leaning back in his chair and gesturing for the man to come closer so he could talk more privately. To this the servant moved nearer bringing his ear much closer to John's mouth. *"Could you possibly be so kind as to check on my missing partner and let me know immediately if there is some kind of a problem,"* John requested, trying not to seem too troubled by her absence.

"Certainly sir, I will see to it at once, will there be anything else Sir?" asked the servant professionally.

"No, and thank you," replied John, in appreciation. The servant then bowed gently, backed away, walked over to the door and left the room.

John then leaned back towards the table and tried to act as normal as possible, knowing that the couple's every move was probably being scrutinised closely by some of the other guests. Within minutes the servant returned and whispered into John's ear. *"Sir, I think you should accompany me at once out into the courtyard,"* he said in a soft calm tone of voice. John looked at the servant in complete shock at the strange request; he was expecting news of Ann merely having to comfort the boy. The servant then gestured with his eyes towards the door but with an expression that suggested that something quite serious was afoot beyond it. To enforce his instructions the servant then took the bold step of moving to help John from his seat. These subtle actions left John in no doubt that he should make his excuses to the Hornbys and quit the room immediately to investigate. John stood up, wiped his mouth with his napkin and took his leave of the other guests with a small bow to either side. He then immediately left the room, accompanied by the servant who hurriedly escorted John outside to the front of the house.

To John's utter amazement, outside the house, he caught Ann in the throes of stepping into a horse drawn carriage. As John approached the vehicle, he watched as Ann then passed a bundle to someone through the opened door of the coach. *That bundle of blankets is our son*, thought John. Ann then stepped inside the post chaise and closed the door. As John and the servant arrived alongside the vehicle, a strange man's voice from inside instructed the coachman to *"Drive on"*. At that precise moment the driver gently tapped the horse's rear with the whip and the carriage went to pull away. *"HALT!"* shouted John as the wheels began to turn but the coachman tapped the horse again. *"HALT I SAY!"* he shouted again, while attempting to hold onto a rear wheel. *"Get to the horse man,"* John then called to the servant

who did as he was told by running forward of the coach and grabbing the horse by the bits. The vehicle was then brought to an immediate stop; held fast by the powerful and firm grip of the large Indian servant. John then stepped up to the rear window where Ann, on the other side of the glass, was beginning to weep. *"What are you doing?"* he asked softly, his heart breaking and tears filling his eyes. *"You don't have to do this,"* he pleaded while gesturing towards the shadowy figure at her side. The mysterious young man then nervously spoke, *" L..,…l…lo… look Ann,"* he stuttered, *"I'm really sorry, but I d, d, don't think I can go through with this any longer."* On hearing this Ann immediately burst into floods of tears. The man grabbed a large bag from beneath the seat; opened the door of the coach, stepped out and walked up the gravel path and into the night; his face obscured by darkness. The young man's identity was of little consequence to John whose eyes never moved from the face of the woman he loved. *"May I come in and talk?"* he gently asked and Ann, with her head in her hands, nodded her consent. John then looked up to see that many of the other guests were now standing on the front steps of the house trying to get a grand view of the event. *"LEAVE US!"* he boomed in their direction, to which they scurried like frightened rats back inside the building.
John then gestured a thank you to the Indian servant who instinctively knew it was his cue to take his leave of the situation. John quietly gave the coach driver his address and then stepped inside and sat down beside Ann. The coach then pulled away as Ann fell into John's arms. *"Shhhh,"* he said tenderly as she begged for his forgiveness. The coach then rolled slowly out of the grounds of the house passing Mr L along the path as it went.

It had taken very little for John to bring Ann back to her senses as she reaffirmed her devotion and joined him at his side once again. The event had shaken John's trust in Ann; his faith and ego had also taken a severe battering. Being an unlucky sort of chap, understandably, he wasn't prepared to take any further chances. As a result he initially took the wise move of placing Ann under the close and watchful eyes of *"a confidential friend of his who received her in a sort of honourable custody".* The whole saga at the Dempster's was explained in the memoirs of John Kemble: *"The India Company, it appeared, had instructed the council to send her back to Europe; but her residence in India would have been connived at, and she might have acquired an immense fortune, if she would have proceeded to Bengal; but her attachment to Captain Haldane seemed then to supersede every other consideration, and she seemed determined to return with him to England. She was, however, another Manon L'Escaut, and the Abbe' Provost might have drawn his heroine from Mrs Cargill. She was preparing to run from the very man, for whom fortune honourably acquired was a cheap and vulgar sacrifice. Before leaving Madras, her protector had been invited to dine with a large party at Captain Dempster's: but entertaining some doubt of the Syren's fidelity, he commanded a trusty servant to pay particular attention to her conduct. As he was sitting down to dinner, his suspicions were confirmed; intelligence was brought to him that an elopement was certainly in agitation. He quitted the room abruptly, and found the fair deceiver just on the point of stepping into a carriage, that had been prepared to receive her by Mr. L, a writer in the Company service. She promised everything for the future, and he forgave her levity.*

It seems that perhaps John Haldane had in fact gained the girl's heart, possibly the very first man to do so. He was also the father of the child whom Ann naturally loved dearly. Some would say, however, that her change of heart probably had more to do with John being from a wealthy and influential Scottish family. Ann's proposed elopement was probably just an attempt at liberation from authority, rather than to gain freedom from John. Given the flippant girl she had always been, she simply hadn't thought about the possible consequences of her actions.

Although Ann was very much an independent woman, eighteenth century India was not a place for any female to be alone. Ann had a scant grasp of the Indian language and certainly had little to no idea of native customs. Travelling across the country, to perform in other major towns and cities, she would have needed a very strong dependable protector constantly by her side and the young Company Writer, Mr L, did not fit this bill. No doubt even he would have been placed under a similar pressure as John, to rid himself of Ann or else face the consequences.

Looking for to see old England,
she prepared to depart.
Aboard the Nancy took her passage,
With heavy purse and light'd heart.
Robert Maybee

6. The *Nancy* Packet

The *Nancy* Packet

The Prime Minister had requested that Ann Cargill, through John Haldane, should be sent home from India and gave them a relatively short time in which to leave. However, John no longer had a ship to command as it was now at the bottom of Bombay Harbour. After the capture of the *Mountstuart* and with the report of the *Fairford's* burning embers still warm in the memory of the Company directors, it was hardly surprising that they were reluctant to hand him another one of their finest vessels. Without an available ship at Haldane's disposal, a very long journey over land was the only other immediate travel option left. This would mean passing through some very unfriendly and even bandit-ridden territories; not exactly a desirable alternative. Without another ship to command, it could be a very long wait for passage by sea back to England. Governor Hornby, understanding and sympathetic to Haldane's predicament as ever, once again came to his rescue. With important news of imminent peace with the warring southern Hindus, (*the Mahrattas)* Hornby desperately needed to get his report of this hastily back to England. The *Fairford* was to have been used for this task but she had been destroyed by fire. When this news reached the East India Company's "*Committee of Secrecy*" they passed a motion to send Hornby another ship. The ship they had in mind had been decommissioned from the Bengal Marine and had stood idle in Cork, Ireland, and was about to be sold off. The ship was called the *Nancy* and the Committee of Secrecy took her under their direct control and sent her to India with the recommendation that she be: *"fitted out in the most expeditious manner"*. The *Nancy* was then converted, in India, from a fighting brig into a mail packet. After her refit she was then described by the Company as: *"a fast express dispatch vessel"*.

The *Nancy* was very much smaller than the ships John had previously been used to but Hornby, under orders of the Committee of Secrecy: *"handed him Command"* and John accepted it gladly; she was very welcome under the circumstances. Built of teak in the Bombay dockyard the *Nancy,* classed as 240 tons burthen, was originally launched for the East India Company on 21st September 1774. She had two masts with a deep draft for off-shore use and mounted ten six pound guns. For ten years the *Nancy* had performed an outstanding service for the Bombay Marine, nevertheless, "*the child of misfortune*" was inadvertently about to put an end to her services.

Like all captains, Haldane would naturally have gone along to inspect his latest charge. At first sight, the *Nancy* would have appeared rather basic. Her topsides were flush decked without forecastle or stern castle, so without the shelter of a quarterdeck, those on watch would be completely open to the elements. Moving aft of the main mast there was a hatchway, surrounded by a handrail, with steps that went down below decks. Further aft was a large twin wheeled helm. Forward of the mast was the ships service, or jolly boat, covered in a tarpaulin and secured to purpose-built holding blocks on deck. From the stern looking forward down the sloping deck, either side of the hatchway, main mast and jolly boat, ten small six pound guns poked out of doorless gun ports on either side. Also between the masts was an all but empty deck area and a small belfry stood just forward in the centre of it. Slightly further ahead of this, just ahead of the forward mast, two solid wooden catheads protruded forwards out at angles on both sides. These held the sheet and best bower anchors firmly to the gunnels of the ship; sheet to starboard, bower to port. Forward of these, and in the centre at the bow, the bowsprit pointed directly ahead from its secure iron mountings on deck, like a lance towards the horizon.

John must have thought the *Nancy* to be a diminutive vessel, probably wondering if perhaps he was in some way being punished for his illicit relationship with Ann Cargill. The ship was quite unlike any of the large two and three decked vessels he was accustomed to commanding; in comparison to those the *Nancy* was like a child's toy. Apart from the ship's general size, her overall woodwork also looked bland and unfussy, lacking the usual show of opulence presented by the elaborate carvings of larger eighteenth century armed vessels. Yes she was small and functional, but she was fast and very sturdily built. No doubt Haldane would have, at some point, placed his hand upon the wood, and in a kind of resigned approval said something along the lines of *"She'll do"*.

From the moment Ann left England, her days in India had been numbered. It was an unfortunate time away in which she must have grown very disillusioned with her celebrity status. Scandal accentuated her fame but it dogged her every move. The general public loved her through it all but those in authority, the wealthy and the powerful, decided her fate. Ann hurriedly put on a benefit performance in order to say farewell to her followers. The show, however, was almost a complete disaster. Even so, this one single performance brought her in *"the astonishing sum of 12,000 rupees"* (1000 guineas. A substantial amount of money in the eighteenth century) Strangely she had chosen an extremely difficult role to play for which she was woefully unprepared. As a result, the audience became restless and she was forced to switch the performance into something more familiar. John Kemble: *"It was solely for her own benefit, for she was totally inadequate to such a character. Her Eliza in the Flitch of Bacon, a little reconciled the spectators to a temperature that was insufferable. The tickets had been put as high as two guineas each, and five hundred persons were too closely collected together."*

Disenchanted but much richer, Ann packed for the journey back to England, probably harbouring thoughts of leading a normal life in Scotland in relative obscurity. Perhaps John had even promised her just such a life near his relations in Gleneagles. That is, of course, if his thoroughbred family were ready and willing to accept Ann Cargill "*the Syren*" with open arms. Given the behaviour of the upper classes towards her thus far, this was highly unlikely.

In early December 1783 the *Nancy* was loaded with stores and dispatches at the Bombay dockside. Also placed aboard was a large wooden box bound in metal strapping and sporting a hefty iron lock. This was Ann Cargill's personal fortune in silver specie along with many expensive jewels she had collected through her life so far; many had been gifts from the men in her life, more from other admirers.

The couple boarded the *Nancy* along with approximately thirty six crewmen and twelve other passengers including a Mr Page, his son and accompanying nanny. John and Ann then left India in the *Nancy* beneath a cloud of scandal as large as the one of smoke the *Fairford* had arrived under. As the *Nancy* exited the harbour it passed close by the wreck site, which was now alive with salvage activity. Unlike the extremely slow trip out on the *Fairford*, the *Nancy* would take only three months to reach English waters and be really quite a pleasurable trip in comparison. Three months of relative comfort in which Ann would be left to reflect on her life and future with John and bond ever more closely with their child. No doubt she was finally becoming more adult. Determined to be a better person, Ann would perhaps even try working harder at keeping the three of them together. John was, after all, the only person to have stood by her since her father, he and their child were also now pretty much the only family Ann had left. Perhaps she finally found in John Haldane a suitable replacement for her estranged parent. Certainly their child made some kind of sense as to what Ann's purpose in the world was really all about; and her life certainly shouldn't any longer entail jumping from stage to stage or from one failed relationship to another. Unfortunately this newfound loyalty and the virtues of motherhood were to be short lived; these were to become Ann's final roles.

Cheerful gales her ship directed,
soon they thought to view our shore.
But alas! the fates ordained,
England they must see no more.

7. St Helena

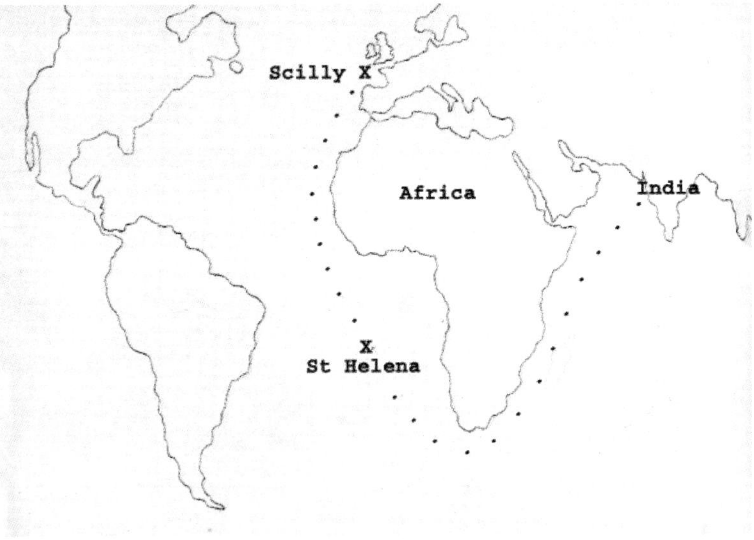

The route to and from the East Indies

Nearly all mail packets, merchant and naval, stop off at British outposts picking up and dropping off mail and provisions on route. Haldane's orders were no different but his visit to Jamestown, on the tiny mid Atlantic island of St Helena, was to prove unique.

A garrison was established by the East India Company at Jamestown St Helena in 1659 and though constantly under threat, the island remained under British control. The island had changed hands on a number of occasions before that date but the East India Company put in a great effort to turn it from a small garrison into a working, growing community defended by a much larger garrison of over four hundred men. As a result, nestled between two tall hills, Jamestown grew into a sizable town. The only thing the island lacked was a decent harbour or anchorage. There was also no quayside, with the only landing place being a shallow wharf, any large vessels were forced to anchor out in James Bay where there was little to no protection from bad weather. The island is little more than seven miles wide by ten miles long and with so many men being garrisoned, there was little for them to do in their spare time but drink; a problem that regularly manifested into violent behaviour. None more so than when the *Nancy* visited the island in the winter of 1783.

The *Nancy* crossed the Indian Ocean and passed by the pirate stronghold of Madagascar unmolested, which was unusual for a lone small vessel but this was probably due to her speed. She rounded the Cape of Good Hope avoiding the Dutch bases in South Africa by keeping well off shore and out of sight over the horizon. Haldane then took his ship out into the mid south Atlantic Ocean. The *Nancy* arrived at St Helena during the Christmas holidays and, being a relatively small vessel dropped anchor just a short distance offshore, in full view of the inhabitants of Jamestown.

The Nancy took up on her anchors amidst the sound of musket fire cracking off in the distance over the nearby town. Knowing from previous experience that all garrisons held regular military manoeuvres and weapons practice, Captain John Haldane acknowledged the sound. He did however, think it a little strange that it was going ahead during the Christmas period but other than that, thought little of it. As others aboard went over to the side of the ship to discuss the noise Haldane ordered the mail bags for St Helena to be fetched up on deck. As this went ahead he then ordered the ship's service boat to be lowered and manned to deliver the mail and despatches ashore. As the boat was being lowered a six oared pinnace, which was earlier seen to leave the wharf side, drew close alongside the Nancy and hove to. *"What vessel are you, who is your Master and what is your business here?"* came a loud voice bellowing from the stern of the vessel. Haldane, immediately thinking this behaviour as most unusual, became mildly agitated by it and this manifested

itself in his reply. *"We, sir,"* replied Haldane indignantly, *"are the mail packet Nancy under the command of Captain Haldane, in the Employ of the Company. Do you not see our flag sir?"* Asked Haldane crossly while gesturing towards the East India Company pennant fluttering gently but in full view aloft.

"Very well, Sir," the man shouted back, *"At the behest of Governor Corneille I beg your indulgence, as the Garrison Commander has requested that you please hold your position for the time being."*

"Is there some kind of a problem?" asked Haldane, eager to conclude his business and feel terra firma under foot once more.

"We will see to your industry directly." The man then reiterated his orders. *"At the request of the Garrison Commander please remain aboard your vessel until further notice."*

This was indeed most irregular, thought Haldane, but did as he was requested by ordering the ship's jolly boat to be hoisted back aboard. Haldane hadn't even been given a time frame to work to, so there was little else to do but await further instruction as requested. As a result Haldane allowed the crew to take their ease and they sauntered about on deck chatting and smoking but paying scant attention to the noise of the musket practice still seemingly in progress ashore. Eventually the noise ceased bringing all eyes towards the town where, twenty minutes later the pinnace again put off towards the *Nancy* laying idle out in the bay. As the boat drew near to the *Nancy's* stern port quarter, so the crew came to that side of the ship to witness proceedings. Again a voice called up from the smaller vessel *"Captain Haldane of the Nancy packet,"* requested a Red coated soldier stepping forward.

"Sir," boomed Haldane back at the man and giving his presence away.

The soldier then acknowledged the Captain by saying *"Major*

Bazzet of the Jamestown Garrison, permission to come aboard Captain?"
"Yes of course, Major," Haldane invited, to which the boat duly drew directly alongside and made fast allowing the Major to climb aboard the larger craft. Once on deck, Major Bazzet saluted Captain Haldane and said, *"Major Bazzet, at your service Captain."* Haldane then offered his hand to shake in a less formal introduction and replied *"John Haldane at yours, welcome aboard Major."* The Major then noticed Ann Cargill as she extended her hand towards him also. *"Ah, forgive me,"* said Haldane in embarrassment, *"this is Mrs Cargill."* Further pleasantries were then exchanged before the Major was allowed to get back down to business. *"Apologies for the delay, Captain, but you are now free to conclude your business ashore. There you may gain all the provisions you wish, compliments of the Governor. You are also invited to dine tonight with his Lordship and the garrison commander, will you accept?"* Haldane looked bemused, as he was expecting a full and immediate explanation at the unusual behaviour towards a company vessel and its crew. *"Yes, of course,"* he said, accepting the invitation but then asked the question that was on everyone else's lips. *"Has there been some kind of problem Major?"* he asked. The Major then answered but his body language made it obvious to Haldane, that it was rather a sensitive issue to broach in public. *"After you have fulfilled your duties, all will be made clear to you by the Garrison Commander."* It was obvious to Haldane from the Major's tone of voice that the man had been issued his orders and would not deviate from them. As a consequence, Haldane pressed the Major no further. *"Please deliver your packages to the wharf side as usual,"* said the Major, before adding *"and would you and the good lady please accompany me aboard my vessel, and allow me to take you ashore*

for a briefing." John and Ann had long since been ready to go ashore, so Haldane issued a few sundry orders to the crew, then, aiding Ann down to the steps, alighted into the Pinnace with Major Bazzet, to go and meet the Governor and the Garrison Commander.

At Governor Daniel Corneille's house, Haldane was delivered the story of a mutinous outbreak that had been occurring in recent days. The incident was extremely serious but it had been brought to a satisfactory conclusion that very afternoon. Corneille explained how the outbreak had been started by a number of disgruntled soldiers and discontent had swept throughout the barracks like a plague. *"Ahh, so that's the reason for all the noise,"* replied Haldane, thinking of what he mistook as musket practice. *"Indeed,"* said Corneille, *"While your ship lay at anchor you were forced to stay aboard until the uprising had been put down. It was rather an anxious time for us when you arrived as, for a short while, the conflict could have gone either way. Understandably an unfavourable outcome could conceivably have placed your ship in grave danger Captain. Sorry you were not better informed but as you can appreciate, we were otherwise indisposed."*

That night during dinner at the Governor's House, Haldane was tentatively asked by Corneille if he would take the ring leader of the mutiny, the very dangerous Sergeant Tooley, back to England aboard his ship. *"This is very irregular,"* replied Haldane with concern *"My ship does not have the facilities to transport dangerous prisoners."*

"We fully understand," said Corneille, *"but Sergeant Tooley was the ringleader and as such is still a danger to the rest of the men, and it's best for all if we can get him off this tiny island and to justice in*

England as soon as possible. Is there no way you can help us with this Captain?" the Governor implored. Haldane felt he was left with no option but to oblige, alleviating Corneille of his problem. After giving the dilemma a little thought, he decided it may be a simple matter to make a cell for Tooley aboard the *Nancy*. *"I suppose we could hold him quite securely in the forward cable locker,"* mused Haldane. *"There is only one way out and changes could be effected to the door latch by my carpenter, so that it can only be lifted from the outside."* The Garrison Commander then spoke. *"I suggest a guard be stationed permanently outside the door, to help keep a close watch on the prisoner."* Haldane nodded in the affirmative but concern showed clearly on his face. The Commander then read Captain Haldane's thoughts and asked, *"Perhaps, with your permission Captain, we should pay a visit to your vessel to best see to the practicalities of the problem, only then would we be able to ascertain the suitability of the accommodation."*
"Yes of course," replied Haldane, *"good idea."*
"First thing tomorrow morning suit you Captain," replied the Garrison commander.
"Yes, fine," said Haldane nodding in agreement, *"come out to the Nancy at nine bells."*

After the Garrison Commander's visit, everything was made ready to accept the human cargo. Thus, as a favour to Governor Daniel Corneille of Jamestown St Helena, the mutinous ringleader Sergeant Tooley was restrained within the forward cable locker of the *Nancy* packet. Here he would spend an uncomfortable trip back to England, where, for his crimes, he was to be made an example of. During the long journey Tooley's only visitors were armed crewmen who, whilst ignoring constant pleas of encouragement to commit further mutinous acts on his behalf, saw only to his most basic of needs.

The mutiny at St Helena was reported in the Morning Herald,

Wednesday 10th March 1784:*"The ill humour of the men was shown first on Christmas day arising from some alterations in the regulations for Punch Houses. On Friday the 26th a riotous body assembled who were for a time appeased by the Governors promises. On the 27th they again became clamourous and finding they could obtain no more supplies of spirits from the Captain of the week, they armed themselves and marched out of barracks with drums beating and fixed bayonets, about two hundred in number, commanded by Sergeant Tooley. The Governor went among them and remonstrated and succeeded in inducing them to return. On Monday 29th the Council removed the grievance about the canteen and directed the Punch Houses to be open as before. In the afternoon the men again became riotous and the Governor secured Sergeant Tooley and marched towards the barracks with the main guard. Before he could reach the barracks a party of the mutineers marched off to the Alarm House firing at Major Grane, who went in pursuit of them. After 10pm Major Bazzett with three officers and 70 men attacked the mutineers at the Alarm House. They were under command of Sergeant Burney and fired on Major Bazzett's party with field pieces but without effect. Musketry was used on both sides for 10 or 12 minutes when the mutineers gave way, 3 being wounded and 103 taken prisoner. Major Bazzett losing 2 killed. The mutineers were all sentenced to death and were decimated. Sergeant Burley and nine others, being shot on 2nd January. Sergeant Tooley was sent prisoner to England but perished with all on board by the wreck of the vessel off the Scilly Islands.* This reference states that Tooley's many accomplices, including Sergeant Burley and over one hundred regular soldiers, were decimated. This is an old Roman term meaning that every tenth guilty man was chosen for the allotted punishment; in this case death by firing squad. It is not clear what example making punishment the East India Company had in mind for the ringleader Sergeant Tooley, but he would never actually come to suffer it.

On cursed Scilly's dreadful rocks,
Neptune then their vessel tossed,
She foundered, split and went to pieces,
Every soul on board were lost.

Robert Maybee

8. Scilly, Anvil of the Atlantic

Scilly, Anvil of the Atlantic
The tall headland in the background stands thirty three metres above tide level

The *Nancy* reached the English Channel in extremely good time but arrived amidst a terrible winter storm that cut visibility down to all but a few yards. Consequently Haldane, inflicted with misfortune once again, failed to gain a proper fix on his position. The marine chronometer had been invented by this time but had not yet been fully accepted as accurate; those that had were still being tested and not to be made widely available for another thirty years. Navigators of this period were still guided across the world's oceans solely by using the sun, the moon and the stars. Due to an extended inability to gain a clear view of the sky above, Haldane was in effect sailing blind using dead reckoning alone. This basically meant he was all but guessing his position. The *Nancy's* position was also later put down to a northwards travelling body of water known at the time as the Rennel current. Further to this, for centuries many charts placed the Isles of Scilly in a position some thirty miles or so to the north. These problems were still in the processes of being overcome or rectified on contemporary charts of Haldane's time. As a result, many more ships than necessary were coming to grief among the Isles of Scilly.

When eventually Haldane established a location of sorts, it was merely from the chance meeting with an unknown vessel that was in a similar situation to that of the *Nancy*. The master of this vessel informed Haldane, across the dividing water between them, that his position was probably much further north than he believed it to be. If Haldane had stuck to his own dead reckoning calculations,with sails reefed for the night, he could probably have continued safely on until daybreak. He could have then gained a more positive fix on his position using the sun the following morning. Instead, believing the Isles of Scilly to lie just a few miles on ahead, he witnessed the other vessel as it came about onto a new heading to south and this left John in a quandary. He could trust his own luck and continue northwards, which unbeknown to him was the route away from danger taking his ship towards the south coast of Ireland, or copy the master of the other vessel and do as he advised and head south. John steered the *Nancy* northwards whilst he came to his decision; no doubt his trail of misfortune having a subconscious affect on his thought process.

In the Captain's cabin Ann was trying to sleep with the baby at her side but John constantly disturbed her as he went over his calculations again and again. As standard practice Haldane had ordered soundings to be taken regularly but each time the depth of water and seabed material sticking to the tallow in the lead, gave no clues that would help his cause. If Haldane had not met with the mysterious vessel, he would probably never have felt compelled to heed the advice given by its Commander. Haldane could have made any number of other decisions, but made what turned out to be the disastrous error of giving the order to bear away to the southeast as advised. Now both the *Nancy* and the other vessel were heading directly towards Scilly; the 'anvil of the Atlantic'. The following record by the Reverend John Troutbeck, written some years later in 1796, shows how the unknown vessel also got into difficulty among the islands, but luckily came to no harm. The *Nancy* however, would not be so fortunate: *"March 4th at midnight there being a very strong gale of wind from the SW and a heavy sea, a transport from New York came in behind the Island of Brehar,* (Bryher) *in such a place as was not possible for any pilot to conduct her through, notwithstanding she never struck one rock, but came safe to anchor. The Captain's name was Robert Bruce, who gave an account to the pilots that he spoke with a pacquet from India, about eleven o'clock that night and supposed she must be lost on some part of the islands".* Unfortunately Master Bruce of the transport vessel from New York was not incorrect. On the night of the 25th February 1784 the *Nancy* had turned southwards into poor visibility. Through a tempestuous sea the ship was tossed about like a cork, its uncomfortable occupants completely unaware of the dangers ahead. Inevitably this resulted in an unexpected rendezvous with the Western Rocks of Scilly. It was late at night with most people aboard already settled down for the night when the *Nancy* ran in amongst the islands. Ann lay in her cot with her arms wrapped comfortingly around the youngster, whilst just across the room John, still wearing his comfortable clothes, was trying to rest; the worry of the ship's position keeping him awake.

Pen or tongue scarce can describe,
The horrors of that dreadful night.
These poor souls saw death before them,
In every form that can affright.
Robert Maybee

9. Self Preservation

Drawn from a relief found on a monument, to Captain John Haldane, in Duddingston Parish Churchyard in Scotland. It is a depiction of the wreck of the *Nancy Packet.* The figure second from the left is clutching what appears to be a baby

Thinking the ship had clear water ahead, no doubt the first mate in charge on deck sailed the vessel, under Haldane's orders, blindly onwards into danger. Soundings had ceased being taken. Unwittingly in the dark, and under poor visibility due to the foul weather, the *Nancy* passed within yards of some very treacherous reefs; the crew in complete ignorance that the ship had passed between the Crim reef and the Bishop Rock. The Retarrier reef could also have easily halted her progress but again she passed with the crew completely oblivious of its existence close by. The only tell-tale sign, which failed to be picked up on by those on deck, being waves that naturally grew much larger whenever the ship passed close to one of these shoals. It was perfectly understandable as the night was dark, the sea rough, visibility limited, and the men were over tired. Inevitably breakers crashing over a taller and more obvious reef were about be sighted. Through the waves the mate saw plumes of white of water breaking around a semi submerged rock dead ahead. With no time to lose, the helm was immediately put hard over to port in order to bear away but it was already too late. As a result the *Nancy* struck the rock violently, pushing in the hull timbers of her starboard side. The rock was called the Gilstone and one of its ragged granite shoulders sent a vehement bone-jarring shudder rumbling throughout the ship. Amazingly, the *Nancy* fell away but immediately started filling with water. The sudden jolt of ship on rock would have shocked everyone below decks into life and almost immediately word came up from below that the vessel was taking on water; and fast:

By the time Ann had stirred into life, John had already grabbed his hat and rushed out the door in his shirtsleeves to get up on deck. Half-asleep and realising there was a problem, Ann looked for her day clothes. At that moment a crewman entered the cabin and shouted at her *"Mrs Cargill, you must get topside immediately, the ship is going down."* With things happening so quickly Ann, whilst still in her nightdress, instinctively grabbed her son and rushed up on deck as so fervently requested. Once there, through driving rain and stinging sea spray, she found John already taking command of the situation; his shouted orders bringing a modicum of relief to her growing confusion and panic. It was wet and bitterly cold on deck, so she hid back down in the hatchway out of the weather and listened to events transpiring outside. All she could hear, however, was Sergeant Tooley kicking violently at the forward cable locker door. *"Help, help, let me out!"* he shouted in panic, his strong Irish accent very evident. Tooley was terrified as the freezing cold seawater was already rising up around his knees. For Ann to free the prisoner, she needed to put down the baby, step down into the rising cold water, then move along the deck in the dark to get to the locker door. Once there it was a simple matter to lift the wooden drop latch to free the imprisoned man. Tooley had no idea that Ann was so close at hand; certainly close enough to set him free but Ann could not bring herself to let go of her child to go to his aid. She closed her eyes in shame and humming to herself tried to blot out the noise of Tooley's pleas for freedom. Tooley could now hear something and he put his ear close to the door to listen. Realising there was a woman singing just out side, he pounded ever harder on the door. *"Hey, Miss, you out there, let me out. Please Miss, please don't let me die in here, please, I beg of you, let me out,"* he pleaded desperately, knowing he must surely be making contact. But Ann just blotted out Tooley's calls by humming even louder.

Wiping the weather from his face John Haldane caught a brief view of land appear a short distance away. With a quick look at the compass he shouted, *"Bear East Nor' East, there's land."*

"East nor East, aye," came the reply from the helmsman. John then turned to Mr Page who was nearby, and trying to be heard above the noise of the weather he said *"Hopefully we can drive her ashore."* Then, looking down at Mr Page's son he found a terrified look on the lad's face. Trying to bring a little comfort he ruffled the boy's hair. *"Don't worry lad,"* he said, smiling and trying to reassure the boy, *"we'll make it alright."* John himself was not quite so optimistic and knew his ship would probably founder long before they got to any land. There was nothing else he could do but continue to bring those around him glimmers of hope. Even with the crew this needed to be achieved by giving out orders to keep them busy. John could not allow anyone to think that all hope was lost. This had the desired affect, as Mr Page turned to his son and said, *"Don't worry, son, when the vessel*

runs aground we can use it as a bridge to get us safely ashore."

The situation was even worse than John had first feared. The sheer weight of rising water down in the hold, caused the helmsman to suddenly shout, *"Captain, the helm won't answer to any command!"* Briefly then, under the force of the wind still being caught in the sails, the ship was almost pushed onto her beam-ends and threatened to turn right over. This signalled to John that the *Nancy* was completely out of his control. He quickly gauged the situation and in a flash of understanding shouted *"Cut all sheets away."* This was done in order to spill the wind being caught in the sails, which in turn should arrest the ship from capsizing. As with all John's orders, the crewmen raced to follow them to the letter, taking knives and hatchets to part all ropes tethering the sails. Many of the men already knew they were just prolonging the inevitable, but a drowning man will do anything just to stay afloat that little bit longer. Instead of just giving up, the men did as they were told.

When all tethered rigging had been cut away, the sails streamed helpless and uncontrollable in the wind; allowing the stricken vessel to slowly settle back into a more upright position. John then took a moment to properly gauge the situation. The *Nancy* was now wallowing aimlessly; her bowsprit dipping into the sea. If they hadn't run her aground by the time the sea had gained on the forward gun ports, all would be lost. Moments later the water was indeed lapping at the sills of the forward gun ports. Seeing this, along with what was left of her sails irretrievably and violently flapping overhead, the scene left John with no choice but to give the command to abandon ship. In his reluctance to shout the order he merely spoke the words to men who were nearest to him *"Ok, men, let's get the boat over the side, it's time to leave,"* he said. As there was only room in the jolly boat for about half the people at most, it was obvious to all that not everyone could get aboard. Shouting above the weather John then said, *"We will get the passengers ashore first, but I need some of you men to remain here until we can come back and get you. Who will stay behind?"* he asked. Bravery in some men forced them to volunteer to remain, others just thought they stood a better chance if they took to the rigging and lashed themselves in. After all, rocks now surrounded the ship, so the water couldn't possibly be very deep. With the people split in two groups, John then chose the stoutest crewmen to man the oars and prepared all the passengers for what lay ahead. Finally, if still reluctantly, he gave the order; *"Well men, it's time to abandon ship!"* he called. It would be the last order he would ever give aboard ship.

The wind slowly turned the *Nancy* side on to the sea and the swell pushed her inexorably on towards Rosevear island. With difficulty the crewmen started dragging the jolly boat over to the leeward side of the ship. Here in amongst the shallows of the Western Rocks, the breakers grew so large that their tops reached into the broken rigging helping the wind to tear the already flapping shrouds to shreds. The rolling water then crashed down across the deck, making progress with the boat slow and dangerous. A crewman, in trying to keep his legs from being torn from under him by the water, held tight on to the stairwell handrail. Here he saw Ann, humming to herself at the bottom of the steps. *"Ma'am, you must come up on deck and get to the boat,"* he urged, but Ann never moved a muscle. *"Ma'am,"* he called again while holding out a helping hand, but still Ann ignored him. The water had now flooded the forward areas including the cable locker where Sergeant Tooley had now fallen completely silent. The freezing water then crept up to touch Ann's bare and shoeless feet. Feeling this she screamed and in utter panic, clambered the steps to get away. As she reached the top step the waiting crewman, still offering his outstretched arm, helped her up on deck. With the baby on one arm, Ann then clung to the handrail with the other. At that moment a huge breaker crashed across the ship. The wall of water forced Ann to her knees but she clung on to the handrail for dear life. The crewman, however, in assisting Ann up the steps, was not holding on. As a result the wave swept his legs away from under him. As he was taken, he grabbed at another crewman for help, unsteadying him, so that both were washed down the length of the ship. The pair then slipped into the sea around the bowsprit. Ann cried out uncontrollably, as the unfortunate men disappeared into the maelstrom.

During the next lull in the sea, the jolly boat was finally lowered over the side. Ann then watched passenger Page as he attempted to get his son and nanny to the boat. His timing was unfortunate for at the critical moment a wave threw them both up against the side of the ship. The nanny was a strong African woman servant and she managed to cling on, but the rushing water washed the much weaker Mr Page out through one of the gun ports. Young Master Page, who was frantically clinging to ropes by the main mast, shouted in terror at the sight of his father being lost to the sea. The view of a parent being taken in front of his offspring was too much for Ann to take, and, in a moment of madness, the sight forced her to again descend the steps of the hatchway. In desperation she turned to do this, only to discover that water was now bulging up just below the opening. At that exact moment, Sergeant Tooley emerged from the water like a corpse stepping from a grave; his cold blue looking face rising from the hatchway opening towards Ann. This spectre of death then stopped as he came face to face with Ann. Both knew she had left him to die but Tooley was in fact very much alive. He stared deeply and coldly into her eyes, his face burning a picture into her soul. Ann closed her eyes tightly expecting retribution and fell to her knees in acceptance of the coming punishment; it never came. When finally she found the courage to look up again, Tooley was gone. *Was he a ghost?* she thought but seemingly without any rational thought, he had leapt over the side.

Death seemed to be at every turn and in her uneasiness Ann buried her face in the bundle of material that encased her son. She clutched the child ever more tightly to her bosom. Inside her head she prayed for deliverance but knew this was only the start of the ordeal. Strangely she found that singing seemed to ease her own suffering, so she attempted to shield herself and the baby from the grim realities all around by again humming a calming lullaby. Consequently, still clinging to the handrail, she fell under the spell of her own voice. And in this way, her mind regressing away from the nightmare, she drifted off into happier times.

At the leeward side of the ship, John and a few men had made progress in filling the boat with people. With crewmen endeavouring to keep the boat alongside, John looked to help those nearest to also climb aboard. These included the African nanny of Master Page and two other men. He then called out for Ann to come to the boat. With water washing around on the deck Ann was on her knees and almost incoherently singing to calm both herself and the baby, seemingly unaware of her predicament. John, realising there was nothing else for it, threw himself towards Ann. He grabbed her and fought his way back over to the boat. After helping to get Ann aboard the jolly boat the nanny pointed towards Mr Page's son, who was still gripping onto a rope at the base of the main mast and pleading for someone to help save him. Initially John wanted to pretend he hadn't heard the pleas, much less notice the quivering youngster. John needed to find the courage to go back aboard a second time. Momentarily the thought of it made him turn his head away. But with conscience biting at his soul, he bravely leapt back aboard the *Nancy*. He made a dash for the boy and grabbed him. Then just as a wave came at them across the deck, almost throwing Master Page at his nanny, John leapt for the boat. At that same moment the jolly boat filled with water but to everyone's amazement it wasn't immediately swamped. Instead, like a chick clinging to its mother, the boat lay alongside the half sunken ship. Frantically bailing out they then managed to push the boat away from the stricken vessel.

The scene was now one of devastation; the deck of the *Nancy* was completely awash and about twenty men were lashed into her battered rigging. For a brief moment, as John had originally wanted, it looked as though his ship might actually drift naturally onto the shore of the nearby island. But to gain that land the *Nancy* would first have to pass over a large area of rising granite called the Rosevear Ledges. Sadly the island was tantalisingly within grasp when the *Nancy* struck violently again, but this time she was held firmly by the reef. Gradually the stern started to slowly settle bringing the bowsprit back out of the water. As the stern slowly submerged a crewman was seen clinging to the helm. Not wanting to let go the water came up around him and breakers forced him to cling on tighter. With the ship now trapped against the ledges, the full force of the waves could take effect hitting the ship harder than before; each wave bringing renewed violence to the vessel. Soon her upper parts were being torn away and slowly the structure was becoming disfigured. Wave after wave relentlessly washed over the ship but still the man at the helm clung on taking the battering. He desperately needed to get aloft but was simply too afraid to let go. Just as he plucked up the courage, a large wall of water tore out the helm and carried it and the man over the deck pushing both hard up against the gunnels. Through the spray John watched as the unfortunate man was crushed between the two. As the wheel fell away, the now severely injured crewman was also taken by the receding water and helplessly dragged down the sloping deck and into the sea astern. Here he tried a last ditch effort at survival by holding onto the stern flag pole. This, however, lasted only briefly, as the sea grabbed the crewman and tossed him about like a rag doll. With his last breath the victim called for help before being pulled under. Seeing this sent Ann sinking ever further into denial as she blotted these violent images out of her mind. She had by now regressed so far that she seemed completely unaffected by such traumatic events. She simply closed her eyes to them and hummed ever louder her lullaby to the baby in her arms.

Scarce had time unto the lord to pray,
that he their lives would save,
ere the vessel went to pieces,
and they found a watery grave.

Robert Maybee.

10. Forlorn Hope

The *Nancy Packet* by James Gillray 1784
(Courtesy of the Isles of Scilly Museum)

If the *Nancy* had settled into deeper water, the men in the rigging would have stood a better chance of rescue because the ship would have held together for a longer period of time. So long as the rigging remained, the sea would just pass over the wreck. As things stood, the *Nancy* was still very much on the surface. Under these circumstances she was being crushed by the sea hard against the rock. In this position the hull would not last very long and the masts would soon fall.

Still bailing frantically those in the jolly boat moved a short distance away from the wreck. Seeing that the ship was going to go to pieces quicker than first thought, John called to the crewmen, who were still clinging to the rigging, to jump, thinking there was more chance of them being rescued if they clung to the sides of the boat. A few dropped into the water but most, out of utter fear, refused to move. Instead they lived in hope that the ship would hold together. The jolly boat was constantly in danger of being swamped again at any moment, or even turned completely over. As a result John wasn't prepared to wait around for very long. *"She's going to pieces,"* he called, *"you must jump now; we can't wait any longer."* John was right, the *Nancy* was collapsing but time and again his pleas went unanswered. After a moment's silence the resigned looks on the faces of the crewmen in the rigging said it all. A voice from a crewman at the bows then called out the inevitable *"Go-go on man, save yourselves."* For a moment John stood in the jolly boat looking in silence at the men in the rigging and they back at him. He then allowed the boat to be moved slowly away and it retreated in the direction of Rosevear island.

As the Jolly boat receded away, its occupants gained a better view of the sheer weight of water now descending over the *Nancy*. Under an almost deafening sound of cracking timbers, the ship collapsed before their eyes; going completely to pieces. Seconds later, she was gone. For a moment the sea seemed to calm briefly as if being appeased, a sight that made the survivors in the boat feel as if they were all destined to live through the disaster; it was a very short respite. During the lull John ordered the jolly boat back towards the wreck site in the hunt for any possible survivors. Amidst items of floating wreckage and Ann's self-preserving humming, a couple of survivors were found and brought alongside. However, returning to its previous violence the sea made it impossible to get the survivors aboard, so they simply clung to the sides of the jolly boat. Unable to hold on for long, one of them succumbed to the freezing bite of the Atlantic Ocean; slipping away unnoticed. Another was saved from being pulled under by the breakers, by the sheer strength and determination of one of the oarsmen.

The jolly boat was now almost surfing in on the swell driven by the wind the short distance to the western shore of Rosevear. As it was pushed ever closer to land, and to what the survivors aboard believed was their salvation, John was struggling to keep some control of the boat's direction. He had decided to make an attempt to get the boat around the far side of the island in order to make a safer landing there; or even make for an inhabited island beyond. John knew that a lee shore is an extremely dangerous place to be in a small boat, as the waves that crash there fall directly onto hard ground. The timing of a landing anywhere on the island, under such difficult circumstances, was critical. The only way to safety, was if the boat surfed in on top of a wave and the people leapt from the vessel the moment it struck the beach. It would then be every man for himself in a frantic scramble up the rocks to safety. This usually involved clutching onto sharp granite in between the breakers which, given the chance, would crush a body hard against the rock or drag it back into the surf. The Western Rocks appeared as a wall of white water, an impenetrable obstacle but John could see a way through to the other side of Rosevear by manœuvring into one of the necks at either side of the island. As this went ahead John shouted instructions on how to stay alive if a safer shore was gained. The trouble was, to Ann, this possibly involved throwing the baby ashore as she jumped to save herself. Ann couldn't even contemplate releasing her child from her grasp, especially not if it involved casting him onto the rocks before the mercy of the sea; in the hope he might survive long enough for someone to reach him. As a result, she just kept on humming to the child in defiance of the circumstances all around her. Everyone was terrified, a feeling that intensified as they were now so close to the shore that they could clearly hear the sound of boulders rumbling around in the surf. Ideally the boat's line of attack through the neck was to head straight into the centre of it. Unfortunately the sea forced the boat closer to a small point on the islands western outer edge. Inevitably the moment came and everyone braced for the coming ordeal. In the trough of the swell, immediately before the wave they needed, the oarsmen frantically started to propel the boat forward. The southern entrance to Rosevear Neck looked so small; a daunting prospect that Ann simply closed her eyes to in terror. The wave should have swept the boat into the neck but at the critical moment the vessel's keel scraped on submerged rocks below. Although only briefly, this halted the boats progress, but it was enough time for the wave to swamp over the stern; the difference between life and death.

With the vessel now awash in the shallows they were at the complete mercy of the sea. Realising the dangers, a couple of men jumped for the rocks on the nearby shore but were immediately lost within the breakers entering the small bay just to port. With the boat now precariously stuck between Rosevear Neck and the bay, in desperation John tried to fend the vessel of the rocks with a gaff. Meanwhile, Mr Page's son, in the stern of the half submerged boat, was being helped by his nanny to cling to his seat. Suddenly the boy caught a view of the Captain's face, which was transfixed by shock at something directly behind the boy. To this the lad immediately turned his head to view

what had so captivated John's attention. He then screamed at the sight and sheer size of the next wave coming at the boat from astern. In little more than an instant the water hit with a powerful downwards force pushing the boat further into the bay and completely capsizing it. Those fighting death either jumped to their fate or were washed from the boat as it was flipped over. Ann, on the other hand, in a kind of acceptance and trance-like state, could still be heard singing to her baby as the boat went over. She disappeared from view with her voice bringing her as much comfort in premature death, as it had fame in life. Mother and child were thereuopon drowned beneath the upturned hull.

It is stated in many reports that no one made it ashore from the wreck, as they were all pounded to death in the surf. William Hickey wrote: *"After a remarkably fine passage they reached the British soundings when a tremendous tempest arose. It being in the depth of winter and they being as it was supposed mistaken in their reckoning, ran ashore upon the rocks of Scilly, where every soul aboard perished"*. However, in the Bath Chronicle, Saturday March 6th, 1784, a report states that one sole was rumoured to have survived to tell the tale of the wreck: *"The Nancy East India packet, which was coming express from, the East Indies, and is lost off Scilly, had the articles of peace as settled in the East Indies on board. The crew consisted of 36 men, besides 12 gentlemen and ladies, passengers, who all perished, they say except one"*.

This reference is interesting, as, for whatever reason, their name still remains a mystery to this day. Certainly, facts like the ship initially hitting the Gilstone before sinking elsewhere, and the people taking to the boat, can only have come from the lips of a survivor or someone else who witnessed the disaster. Reports do exist, one of which is in the Whitehall Evening Post on the 9th March 1784, stating that the *Nancy* packet: *"was seen to go down by a Revenue Cutter."* If this were the case, then why did the cutter not go to their aid. We assume this reference to be suspect, as the general consensus is that it was a full seven days before anyone ventured out to the wreck. With that in mind, one is then led to ask a burning question regarding the survivor; why was that person's name never recorded? Was that person so traumatised by the disaster that they suffered memory loss enough to forget their own name? Or was it that the survivor was actually someone who did not want their name to be known; someone who had nothing to lose but everything to gain from the unfortunate event; someone who would benefit greatly from complete anonymity; Sergeant Tooley was just such a person.

For someone like Tooley to survive a disaster such as that which drowned the rest of the *Nancy* packet victims, he would first need to understand a few things about being shipwrecked. One of the first things he would have understood to be imperative, was to discard his boots and any heavy items of clothing before entering the water, as such items are notorious for causing many deaths at sea. This is because the weight of shoes, boots etc will eventually drag a person under. Like anyone in a similar situation, Tooley would have had the understandable urge to make land as quickly as possible. However, in this predicament he would have needed to overide that urge and seek better options to land in a relatively safer enviroment. The next thing he needed to do was to try to get to a small but controllable bouyant object. A large bouyant object is better if one is lost out in the open ocean but it must be discarded when nearing a lee shore. A survivor like Tooley needed to avoid the lee shore of Rosevear at all costs, his best route to survival being to make for the far side of the island; therefore, if unable to swim, he needed to maintain control over his bouyant object to achieve this aim. Only then would he be able to manoeuvre himself around the island to land safely. Haldane would have faced similar choices in the jolly boat. The only difference between the Captain of the *Nancy* and a survivor like Sergeant Tooley, is that ill fate always attended John Haldane!

Drove to land by foaming billow,
On shore was found poor Cargill's clay
Clasped within her lifeless arms,
Her tender infant then it lay.
Robert Maybee

11. Cargill's Clay

Nancy Porth, viewed looking towards the south. Scattered around this cove is where most of the victims bodies were found.

On the morning of the 26th February mailbags started drifting ashore on St Agnes alerting the locals to the wreck. These were picked up and handed over to the local customs officers Edward Rogers and William Harvey who immediately organised their delivery to Nathaniel Smith Esq, Chairman of the East India Company Directors: *"Sir, the Nancy Packet Capt Haldon(sic) from the East Indies with all aboard her having been lost on the Rocks of Scilly on the night of the 25th inst. & meeting with a letter adressed to you, also some for other Gentlemen of the East India House with many others I thought it advisable to inclose the whole for your inspection. I have also sent two Bills of Exchange which fell into my hands loose. I am Sir your most Obedt Servt Wm Harvey".*

(The above letter is dated 27th February 1784 and is the best reference the author's have yet seen for the date of the disaster which has previously been misreported.)

As is usual in such circumstances the local men then set off in search of the wreck to rescue any survivors at the earliest opportunity. On this particular occasion they struggled to find a full crew. A Mr James Herne from London, who was simply holidaying on Scilly at the time, volunteered to fill the empty seat. He was simply on hand and willing to help. For a gig to take a stranger along wasn't the only unusual circumstance to surround this particular rescue attempt. Many times in the history of Scilly it has been recorded how the local men put to sea in gigs to successfully rescue victims of countless disasters at sea. Another job they performed well, generally under very difficult conditions, was to bring ashore any dead they found, allowing them to be given a proper burial. This time was to be different. This time, with the well-intended interference of Mr Herne, it would become a somewhat botched job.

Following the trail of wreckage, the St Agnes gig and its crew were inevitably led out to the Western Rocks. They passed through the Neck of Rosevear where, on the seaward side of the island, they met with a terrible scene of devastation. Bodies, wreckage, flotsam and jetsam appeared to be everywhere. Instinct took over as the men's eyes then scoured the rocks for any survivors. They also called out hoping to gain responses from the living, but after much searching, they found only the silence of the dead. A little bay on the west side of Rosevear island, now referred to as *Nancy Porth,* was discovered completely filled with wreckage; so much so that the water's surface was all but obscured. Amidst this carnage the upturned jolly boat was seen to be afloat on the surface; the thin curving keel of its bow pointing skywards. A gig ventured into the porth and searched among the wreckage for even the faintest signs of life but found only naked disfigured bodies. The boatmen then went on to the island to search it on foot but again only mutilated bodies were found littering the rocky shoreline. After all hope of survivors was given up, the crew of the gig started to bring the bodies and some of the wreckage ashore. The corpses were carefully carried up the rocky incline and laid out on the ground. The victims needed burying, but there were too many and no tools had been brought for such a job. Mr Herne then offered payment to whomever would perform the task.

Meanwhile, down in Nancy Porth, a line had been attached to the upturned boat in order to get it into the shallows. Once there other men waded out to the boat to right it again. Together they got their hands beneath the gunnels and lifted the boat over. There, beneath the vessel, they found a melancholy scene to break the strongest heart among them. Ann was found dead, floating face up in the water, with the infant still clutched tightly in her arms. Whilst many other victims bodies were badly damaged by the rocks, or found only partially clothed at best, the up-turned boat had served as some protection against the sea. Neither mother nor child had been badly disfigured and both were found still wearing their nightclothes. The only damage reported to the bodies of either Ann or the child was written many days later in the Morning Herald 10th March 1784: *Mrs. Cargill's body was one of the first that came on shore, which looked extremely well, except that one of her breasts was shockingly torn".* (At this point in the story Ann Cargill's body had not yet been identified as such at Scilly.)

Ann's eyes were closed and her cheek was resting on the infant's head as if merely asleep. They would have looked strangely serene if it were not for the fact that both their faces were the palest blue grey and the boy's eyes were wide open. Although glazed over white, the boy had a completely cold and deathly gaze that seemed to stare straight into infinity. Further to this, created by the movement of the water, Ann's long dark hair moved about in a kind of slow motion, as though being blown about on the wind. The flimsy white attire worn by the pair also appeared to make them seem alive; it billowed in and out in the swell, flowing in gentle waves of motion over their bodies. This all made an already rather morbid scene all the more macabre; seemingly giving their lifeless corpses a curious animation. Unwilling to witness the scene any longer, one or two of the men felt compelled to turn their heads away, whilst others took off their hats and penitently crossed themselves over the scene. John

Kemble: *"This lovely creature was found floating in her chemise, as she had lain in her bed, and in her arms, inseparably clasping, the infant of which she had been delivered. The maternal instinct had not yet yielded even unto death itself."*

Seventeen bodies were found by the rescuers, including young Master Page. The others were never found. All those recovered were carried onto the top of Rosevear island and laid out among the lush green mallows that grow there. One by one, Mr Herne took accurate descriptions of those that were still recognisable. The Captain was probably identified by items of clothing, such as a distinctive red neckerchief, that still hung from his lifeless body. Shallow graves were then dug and the bodies were placed into them. Either through chance or deliberate selection, the bodies of Ann, her son and possibly John Haldane were given the deepest graves. These were dug into natural fissures in the bedrock. For the rest of the bodies, because the earth was found to be only a foot or so deep at best, it was all the men could do to cover them with a thin layer of sod and hide what was still on view with loose rocks and stones. A very basic ceremony was then performed over the scene before leaving. John Kemble*: "Her body had been seven days underwater. Her remains were buried at Scilly, by a private gentleman, at his own expense; and at his charge were interred fourteen of her fellow sufferers and two infants. He caused as accurate descriptions as could be taken of the bodies to be drawn upon the spot, and carried a copy of them to London himself, to assist the friends of the parties in ascertaining their loss."* It is clear from this and following references that about seventeen bodies were interred on Rosevear island after this one single disaster; thus proving that human remains were on the island to be found later on. A few of these bodies, however, would eventually be removed which we will come to later. It is interesting to note that two infants were buried suggesting that Ann could have been separated from her son and that, although unlikely, they had prised the boy from her maternal grasp and buried them apart.

The mailbags which had floated free from the wreck, continued to come ashore and these contained some very important documents that needed to be delivered to East India Company offices in London. Mr Herne offered to take these documents himself when he returned to the city. Mr Rogers of the Customs agreed and allowed the mails to be placed in his charge. Reverend Troutbeck in his Survey of the Islands in 1796 wrote:*" The mail was taken up by the islanders and sent to London by Edward Rogers Esq. Collector of the Customs, and Mr James Herne, from London, here at the time for pleasure."* (During research the author's have indeed seen East India Company documents in the British Library which were signed by Governor Hornby and sent from Bombay Castle in late 1783. These documents, however, are mostly written in code.)

At this time the names of victims, such as Ann Cargill, were still unknown. Although shortly after the burials had taken place on Rosevear, from documents recovered from the wreck, the passengers names were finally ascertained. The "*person*" described in the following narrative was probably one of the Customs officers: *"A person whose business is to attend at the Scilly Islands, on seeing some letters washed on shore, which, on opening, he found came from India, suspecting some vessel from that part of the world to be lost, offered a large reward for any person to go off; they accordingly discovered the wreck underwater with great difficulty, and got up a packet bag, which contained several letters. The following are part of the passengers known to have been on board the Nancy at the time; Mr Percy, Surgeon to Sir Edward Hughs; Mr Ashburner; late of the council of Bombay; Mr Bond; Mr Page and son; Miss A. Thomson; Captain Haldane; his first and second mate; Mr M'Kenzie; Mrs Cargill, and an infant child of twenty months old. The bodies were mostly naked, and supposed to have been in bed at the time."*

The Gentlemen's Magazine provides a more accurate number of the victims giving: *"that her crew were 36 in number and that there were 12 passengers".*

So peace be to her precious soul,
tho' dreadful was her timeless fate.
We hope the lord her sins forgave,
and now she is in blessed state.

Robert Maybee

12. Re-committal at Old Town

Old Town Church
(Screen print by Helena Wakefield)

When news of the victims true identity became common knowledge on the Isles of Scilly, the information eventually found its way to those who mattered. No doubt many islanders thought it shameful that among those hastily buried on Rosevear, in unmarked graves and denied a proper Christian burial, included the famous and celebrated actress Ann Cargill. The men that buried the bodies, under the instructions of Mr Herne, had no idea who the people were and simply did what they thought best at the time. However, the saga became an embarrassing and unfortunate fact that needed immediate rectification. Consequently, a Captain Scott, whose ship was temporarily laid up at Scilly, took to small boats with his crew to recover the bodies. They also took along the local men who had originally recovered the bodies from the sea. On Rosevear island the locals assisted Scott to the position of the graves and there they uncovered Ann and all the other corpses. Only three were found to be in reasonable enough condition but one of the more intact bodies was identified and recorded as being that of Ann Cargill. The rest of the victim's bodies had, for want of good earth, only been covered with rocks and stones. These were reported by Scott as *"too far gone with putrefaction to be removed."* As a result, he elected to re-bury them and leave them behind on Rosevear. In the report made by Reverend John Troutbeck, it states that: *"Several dead bodies upon the said island, amongst which was the body of Mrs Cargill. One Captain Scott, belonging to Hartlepool, stranded here at the time, bound to London from Cork, laden with butter, hides etc. with some of his ships company went to the island of Rosevere (sic) and took up the body of Mrs Cargill and two more, and brought them to St Mary's."*

Although Ann's body was definitely removed to St Mary's, it is not entirely clear who the other two recovered victims were. Although those who believe in the supernatural would like to think that Ann's ghost haunts Rosevear island because she is searching for her lost child, it is unlikely that the baby was separated from Ann during the initial burial. This brings us to conclude that the child was also buried with Ann in Old Town Churchyard. We also believe that the third body brought back to St Mary's was that of John Haldane but have not as yet been able to prove this emphatically. However, one need only point towards the fact that, not only was John Haldane known to be the Captain, he was also from an important and wealthy family whose, "of Gleneagles" lineage goes back through centuries of Scottish history. The Haldane's would have no doubt been very upset had his body been left on the lonely remote Island of Rosevear.

The three recovered corpses were conveyed to St Mary's where a proper service in Old Town Church took place. The parson then presided over the interment in the graveyard somewhere to the south side of the church. Throngs of islanders undoubtedly turned out to see the committal of the celebrity. It would no doubt be the closest any of them would ever come to one so famous. If the equivalent circumstances happened today regarding a modern celebrity with similar talent and popularity having died among these tiny islands, the interest would have been exactly the same. Kemble laments: *"This melancholy expiation of all her errors left a tender regret for her loss, which outlived the usual duration of such tributes to the public favourites."* The Times Newspaper also reported: *"A neat monument has been erected at St Mary's one of the Isles of Scilly in memory of Mrs Cargill. It is said to have been paid for out of the produce of some jewels that were found upon her."*

Accounts of Ann's death with an infant clutched tightly to her bosom certainly made her a tragic figure for the press and the media descended on the islands to get a better grasp of the tragic story. However, the saga was all but over by the time any reporters arrived and the key participants, such as Captain Scott and his men and the aforementioned "*private Gentleman",* Mr James Herne, had left the islands. The fact that Ann had actually been buried, exhumed and re-buried, was kept from the press for obvious reasons. Moreover, the above memoirs reporting that the memorial had been paid *for "out of the produce of some jewels found upon her"* is also quite likely to be inaccurate, as all other reports described her as being found: "*floating in her bedclothes*". It was more likely that a fund was set up by the Islanders to pay for everything and that during the time between the wreck and the funeral, locals had salvaged some of Ann's jewels from the wreck. These jewels could have been, with either guilty conscience or good intent, handed in to the fund and used to pay for the memorial. Naturally the press would have been given a different story to hide the fact that salvage had taken place over what must, at that precise moment in time, have been viewed as a mass grave. The new wreck site would certainly have been viewed as extremely sensitive. The *Nancy* was after all a tomb and those removing items from it perceived by many as little more than grave robbers. The press would have had a field day had they spoken to all the right people and shame could have been heaped upon the islanders by the press. Fortunately this was averted, with all the unfortunate circumstances being hidden for more than two centuries. Another myth that would not be dispelled for over two hundred years, due to misrepresentative contemporary newspaper reports of the period, was that: *"the Nancy was wrecked on Rosevear island"* and not on the Rosevear Ledges where she had in fact sunk. Not an unreasonable error by any means, but one that would make any later searches for the wreck more difficult.

Rosevear Ledges at low tide in the foreground. Viewed looking west towards the Gilstone which is the tallest rock in the background.

The picture opposite is taken from the top of Roesvear looking towards the southeast

Different ways grim death attacks us,
youth and age before him fall.
Let everyone prepare to meet him,
none can tell when he will call.
Robert Maybee

SECTION (3)

1. Aftermath

The modern day Bishop Rock Lighthouse.
A legacy of disasters like the Nancy packet.

News of the disaster eventually filtered its way through to the Royal Society in London, where one of its members, Major James Rennel, attempted to explain the reason for the loss of the *Nancy* packet. The Rennel current, an interesting phenomenon discovered by the Major, was squarely blamed in his address. No mention was made of the inaccuracy of charts of the period, even though these were as equally to blame by giving a position of the Isles of Scilly as much further north than they actually were:

"The public is much indebted to Major Rennel for explaining the cause why ships, in coming from the Atlantic, and steering a course for the British Channel, in a parallel south of the Scilly islands, often find themselves to the North of those islands. The prevalence of westerly winds in the Atlantic impels the waters along the north

coast of Spain, and accumulates them in the Bay of Biscay; from which they are projected along the coast of France in a direction N.W. by W. to the westward of Scilly and Ireland. It is to this formerly undescribed current, that we are to impute the loss of the Nancy packet in our own times, and that of Sir Cloudesly Shovel, and others of his fleet, in the beginning of the present century; besides numberless cases equally melancholy, but of less celebrity. The Major, in a paper read before the Society, explains the means by which such disasters may be avoided in future." Modern studies have found no evidence of the current discovered by Major Rennel. However, there are North Atlantic currents which are known to shift position periodically, therefore it would be wrong to state that it never existed back in 1783-4.

Such was the furore caused by this latest shipwreck disaster that questions were even asked in Parliament by the Admiralty and the East India Company. *"The ill fame of the Scilly islands, for the losses they have occasioned to navigation has been known even to children."* These words, written by Benjamin Tucker, Surveyor General to the Duchy of Cornwall, were a view that was also conveyed to His Royal Highness the Prince of Wales in Tucker's scornful report. Tucker was petitioning for lighthouses to be built on the Isles of Scilly, including the one on the Bishop Rock. He mentions no less than 34 ships wrecked within a very short space of time. He goes on to make a direct reference to the *Nancy* packet disaster. It is therefore highly likely that this shipwreck in particular was the catalyst that directly initiated plans for the Bishop Rock Lighthouse being drawn up: *"...we ourselves recollect the loss of the Nancy packet with all the crew and passengers including Mrs Cargill. What then will be the reflections of that man, to say nothing of his responsibility to the country, who shall delay the execution of the plan recommended, for even one winter, should it prove that in that period any other vessels, either of our own or other nations trading with us, shall have perished for want of lighthouses!*

Governments being what they are, it would still be decades before that fantastic feat would be accomplished. It was then perhaps ironic that the men constructing the Bishop Rock Lighthouse would make the macabre discovery of some of the victims of the *Nancy* packet, a very grim reminder as to why the work was being undertaken.

It is interesting to note that in 1808, the period between the *Nancy* victims being shabbily interred on Rosevear, and before the lighthouse project began, an act of Parliament was passed called the Grylls Act. The Grylls Act dealt with the procedures regarding the burials of bodies cast up by the sea and the Act states that: *All bodies cast ashore must be recorded and given a Christian burial in consecrated ground, regardless of Race, Creed or Colour.* No wonder the most Christian among the lighthouse workmen on Rosevear became so worked up about moving the remains. The *Nancy* debacle clearly had far-reaching effects.

We saw her treasures cast away,
The rocks with pearl were sown,
and strangely sad, the ruby's ray
flashed o'er the fretted stone.
Unknown author

2. Braithwaites Visit to Rosevear

John Braithwaite

Although the islanders have salvaged from shipwrecks from when man first took to exploring the worlds oceans, Scilly has attracted divers and salvagemen from the mainland for centuries. In 1750 John Lethbridge descended in an engine to salvage from the wreck of the *Association* lost in 1707. The "*engine*" was really a sealed barrel with a viewing port and leather sockets from which his arms protruded. Then there was Mr Enoch Tonkin who came to salvage guns from the wreck of the *Colossus* in 1798, using an engine of an unknown design. Next were the Deane brothers, who came to Scilly in 1828 and salvaged a cargo of elephant tusks from a brig called the *Hope.* The Deanes' equipment was the forerunner of the now familiar standard helmet design which revolutionised diving and was adopted by salvagemen and divers the world over. There have been many other divers to follow in this long tradition and the wreck of the *Nancy* was about to meet with its eighteenth century pioneering salvagemen, the Braithwaite family.

By the summer of 1784 the dust had all but settled and local men felt comfortable enough about the situation over the wreck to set about salvaging from the site once more. They relocated the *Nancy* and attempted to reclaim what they could. This work was performed from boats with tools from above the waters surface and to limited effect. However, when summer came it brought with it a professional salvage team who had come to work the wreck in a more serious manner by physically descending down to it. These salvagemen were the Braithwaites and along with their machine, they had beaten rivals like Mathew Cox and another unnamed diver to the wreck, even though both these rivals had written to the East India Company properly seeking the contract: *"Seeing an account in the papers of this day, there were 200,000 in Jewels and specie on board the Nancy, I take the earliest opportunity to inform you that I have copper diving dresses to visit the unfortunate ship, with proper tongs & C for bringing up what may be comeatable (sic), am willing to undertake the business on salvage with an allowance for expences, the sooner the business is undertook the greater the possibility of succeeding. am your most obedient servant Mathew Cox.*

Cox was clearly after the treasure whereas the other unnamed diver, simply referred to as a Lieutenant in the East India Company employ, was looking to raise the entire vessel if at all possible. A Mr John Harriett wrote to the East India Company on his behalf: *"As a servant duty bound to render any & every service in his power to those from whom he receives his principal support, your humble servant, a Lieutenant on half pay, takes this liberty of in forming you that on perusal of the loss of the Nancy Packet from bombay, he is humbly of the opinion that his judgement, grounded on experience relative to raising sunken vessels, or if too much wreck'd to be raised entire, in getting up the goods &C from the broken parts of the wreck, may be of service by going down & examining the abovementioned Packet."* It is unclear if the Braithwaites, the men who had already arrived at Scilly, had sought any permission to work the wreck; not that it was necessary just courtesy, as salvage laws allowed anyone to take to salvaging.

John Braithwaite was actually a fire engine maker by profession and a very determined individual with two rather talented sons, William and John. William was an ingenious mechanic who won a gold medal from the Society of Arts for the best model of a crane; and John, an accomplished sculptor, received a medal from the Royal Academy for his work.

Diving and salvage was still rather primitive in the late eighteenth century but one need only look briefly into the Braithwaite's past salvage record, to understand just how capable these men became in developing an expertise in this particular field. All that is known about their actual diving equipment is that it was bulky and peculiar and fed with air at normal surface pressure through a connecting leather hose. There has in fact been much debate among historians as to whether the Braithwaites equipment was in fact merely another diving bell. However, the evidence at Scilly may point towards the equipment used here as being something else, as a bell could not possibly have been used in the position where the *Nancy* was lost. Further to this the following description by an unknown author, not only gives some clue as to the equipments usefulness, it also emphatically states the apparatus as being a chamber peculiar unto Braithwaite and not just another diving bell: *"The nature of this artist's apparatus is peculiar unto himself; his general practice is to remain underwater for six hours consecutive. He declares he could without inconvenience remain in his chamber underwater for six weeks, or any length of time."* Equipment was indeed used to great success on many occasions and in many other parts of the world. The Braithwaite family raised great bronze and iron guns from Spanish gunboats lost off Gibraltar; and were rewarded in North Africa after gifting six great iron guns from a wreck to an African Prince. They went on to raise ordinance from the submerged naval losses of the *Royal George* in Portsmouth; the *Venerable* of Torbay; the *Colossus* in the Isles of Scilly; and raised much from the wreck of the *Earl of Abergavenny* lost in Weymouth Bay. However, given the position of the Nancy, close in amongst the rocks and tides of the Rosevear ledges, casts serious doubt that a large vessel needed to operate a bulky diving bell, could have anchored safely and in close enough over this particular shipwreck, in order to perform effective salvage work. To perform this particular salvage the Braithwaites equipment needed to be more manoeuvrable than a bell and therefore remotely operational from the mother vessel above. Further to this, a letter presented on the opposite page, also describes the Braithewaites equipment not as a bell, a well known piece of diving equipment that had been employed by many over previous centuries, but as a *"Machine"*. When taken within the historical literal context within which it was written, the word *Machine* means: *Vehicle; with moving parts.*

To gain the aforementioned salvage contracts, the team first needed to impress as they were entering into competition with many other salvage outfits. The Braithwaites earned their reputation by working sites like that of the *Nancy* packet. This was probably as a result of the *Nancy* having been deemed as a relatively easy target; her guns etc were small in size and therefore viewed as easy to recover. Ann Cargill's personal fortune was also an attraction. The Gentlemen's Magazine of 1784 reported that the *Nancy* carried: *"money and jewels on board to a great amount."* A further report during that same year appeared in the monthly London Magazine and it also stated Ann's fortune as being *"200'000 in specie and jewels."* If located, this money was a rather tantalizing bonus to any salvage outfit and one that must have given great encouragement to visit the Isles of Scilly.

The Braithwaites would have arrived hoping that the treasure still remained within the wreck. However, given the fact that Ann's funeral was paid for using some of her own jewels, it is possible that the locals may have already removed some, if not all, of the treasure. If not, weather permitting, the Braithwaites were certainly more than capable of doing so.

We know nothing of the results of the Braithwaite's summer salvage of 1784. However, an unknown author does give a vivid account in a letter, of the Braithwaite's initial location of the wreck site. What is very interesting about the following letter, is the passage about their subsequent visit to Rosevear island. We must remember that in Braithwaite's time there were not yet any buildings on the island, only nesting birds with the pungent smell of ammonia from guano covering the rocks. As the men made their way through the thick tree mallows, whilst all the while being dive bombed by resident sea gulls, they inadvertently stumbled upon some partially exposed human remains: *"Everything is at present very scarce here, of account of the long drought, as we have not had any rain since the beginning of May. What provisions we get are brought from*

Land's End, and when it arrives here, it is almost stinking. There is a sloop in the harbour, with the ingenious Mr Braithwaite and his two sons on board, who sometime ago took up an anchor to the Royal George. We went with them about four leagues, to the westward of this place: to a small uninhabited island called La Roche Verde, or green rock, (Rosevear) *where the Nancy Packet was lost on her return from the East Indies, where the unfortunate Mrs Cargill perished. Some distance from the shore the younger Mr Braithwaite went down in his machine, and remained two hours underwater, but could not meet with anything although the inhabitants of the islands have at different times found many valuable articles driven*

on there. Whilst on the island, we saw great quantities of bones of the Nancy's crew, covered, with small trusses of grass. This was a melancholy spectacle to us, on recollecting the sudden fate of our unhappy countrymen, who, in the moment they were comforting themselves with the prospect of returning to their friends, were, alas! suddenly sent to that undiscovered country from whose bourne no traveller returns."

It is clear from the preceding letter that Captain Scott had not properly replaced the rocks back over the remaining victim's bodies, as the vegetation was now growing through and around some of the exposed bones. It is also interesting to note how easily the remains were found, and importantly, during just one visit. This fact gives further credence to the lighthouse workmen who are believed to, and most assuredly did, rediscover the same remains some fifty or so years later. It is also an interesting fact that the above refers to the island as the *Roche Verde* when it was known as Rosevear at that time. This was simply because the Braithwaites were no different to modern day treasure-hunters and salvage men. They simply preferred to keep the actual positions they worked a secret. Perhaps it was the Braithwaites who gave Rosevear the name *Roche Verde*.

Did the Braithwaites work the wreck for long? Well, with the capability of remaining submerged for over six hours at a time, it is unlikely that they simply left without salvaging anything from the site at all. Unless of course the wreck was too deep for them or conditions forced their premature withdrawal. There are in fact very few days each year in which the sea will allow any visitor out to the Western Rocks of Scilly. However, it must be considered since the letter above states the Braithwaites' visit was in mid summer, during a long drought, which usually means an extended calm and settled spell of weather. This must surely suggest that the sea conditions were very conducive to salvage work. Furthermore, with the logistics involved in getting themselves and their equipment to Scilly, they must also have allocated themselves a substantial amount of time in which to complete their intended task. A month to six weeks of time that encompassed August, traditionally the calmest month of the year, is an entirely reasonable assumption.

Nothing more can be added to this part of the story other than to reiterate the numerous tales of people, while in the vicinity of Rosevear island, claiming to have heard mysterious music; the best of which emanates from the lighthouse construction workforce and was referenced in an earlier chapter. However, these tales passed over into folklore; Ann Cargill's extraordinary life story also moved into history. Any inscriptions on her monument faded away with time. Eventually the very structure of her tomb in Old Town Churchyard fell into disrepair and, in crumbling condition, was probably removed. Similarly, the mass grave on Rosevear island became completely obscured by overgrowing shrubs and all the now obsolete buildings became the ruins we see today. Apart from the occasional inaccurate report written in modern literature about the *Nancy* packet, the ship and her fascinating story were all but forgotten. The true position of the wreck was lost, with the site becoming contaminated with wreckage of other later vessels suffering a similar fate over on the Rosevear Ledges.

And Gold was strewn the wet sands o'er,
Like ashes by a breeze,
and gorgeous robes, -but oh! that shore
had sadder sights than these.
Unknown author

3. Eureka

Ed

Todd

Carmen

Phil

Paul

James

Robin

Ed Cumming 40 years dive experience - Author\Chemist.
Todd Stevens 30 years dive experience - Author\Carpenter.
Carmen Stevens 20 years dive experience -Guest house owner.
Phillip Roberts 20 years dive experience - Engineer.
Paul Stevens 25 years dive experience.- Dental Technician.
James Fletcher 5 years dive experience - Conservator
Robin Burrows 10 years dive experience - Technical Whizzard.

Co author Ed Cumming is a very quiet, unassuming type of chap but beneath the surface lies something much more adventurous. This showed itself to be evident when he and his wife Barbara took the decision to relocate to Scilly from Weymouth in the autumn of 2005; and immediately joined a local band of dedicated divers. Retired chemist, Ed, like myself, is an old school diver with many years experience. There are also other similarities between us. Not only do we both share a fascination for diving and shipwrecks in general, we had both raised vast collections of material from eighteenth-century shipwrecks for public display; the *Earl of Abergavenny* and *HMS Colossus* respectively. We have also both accepted archaeological awards for our previous works. However, unlike myself, Ed had amassed a mountain of thorough and extensive research surrounding no fewer than four other wrecked East India Company ships. In the short time Ed had been on Scilly, it became obvious to us all that, through his investigative abilities, he was an extremely thorough individual and a man not to be taken lightly.

Before the inclusion of Ed, the dive team at this time consisted of three regular members: Phillip Roberts, Carmen Stevens and myself. There was also Paul Stevens, Robin Burrows and James Fletcher who joined the team as and when they could. During this period the team were finishing work on our latest project; a rare 19th century shipwreck we had only recently discovered in amongst the Islands. So rare in fact, that the Government were about to place a protection order upon the site. Inevitably, this was signalling an end to our involvement with the wreck, so Ed's timing in interesting us with another project was going to be perfect.

During the autumn of 2006, Ed visited my home asking for suggestions of a local project for him to get his teeth into. He was particularly interested in wrecks linked with the English East India Company, so one or two local shipwrecks immediately sprang to mind. Little did I know how the one finally suggested was about to take off. *"How about the Nancy packet?"* I asked, knowing the wreck to be an East India ship, and one that carried Ann Cargill's personal fortune on board. Furthermore, the remains of the *Nancy* had not yet been positively identified and I had a good idea that the history behind the ship was potentially very interesting. The *Nancy* had also been suggested as the team had already been taking a modicum of interest in locating what remained of her during the previous season. That search had been carried out along the western shoreline of Rosevear island, as current documentation stated the wreck had been lost there. Initially Ed placed the wreck on a list of possible things to do but eventually, in winter 2006, the *Nancy* packet made it to the top of the pile. He then made a concerted effort to look into the ship's history; it was a tale that pulled him in heart and soul. Soon he had amassed a large amount of research material from a wide spectrum of sources. The story Ed unearthed became so fascinating, I had no option but to take notice of anything he had to say about the *Nancy* packet, especially when he said he had a viable position in which he believed her remains could be found. This news was about to make the team drop any other ideas we had for new projects, in favour of a more intensive effort to search for the *Nancy* packet.

Ed is the sort of individual who when he finds something new or of interest, he cannot wait to share it with someone else. *"Todd,"* he said enthusiastically one day at his home and said like it was his eureka moment *"I think I've got it."* He then gave a brief resume of his findings. *"Look,"* said Ed, passionately, *"all current references show the ship as having hit the Gilstone before being driven onto Rosevear."*

"Yes," I replied, knowing that team members, including Phil, Carmen and myself, had already used these same references to search the western shore of that island; our only discovery that time being an anchor that was too late in date to be from the wreck of the *Nancy*.

"Well look at this." said Ed, handing over some documents contemporary with the disaster; one of text about a salvage shortly after the wreck had happened; a photograph of a memorial stone in a churchyard in Scotland; and lastly, a black and white copy of a contemporary narrative of the disaster itself. Ed referred

enthusiastically to the narrative as "*the Gillray Print.*" *(See front cover picture and explanation overleaf)* The print caught my attention as, although a copy, it was clearly a dated piece of artwork that anyone viewing it would find wonderfully evocative. After casting an eye over the photograph of what looked like an obelisk, I then read the short text on the documents. The point, however, went completely unnoticed as I failed to pick up on what Ed was getting at. *"Fantastic picture"* I said, *"where did you get it? "Never mind that, look at it again,"* he said, with excitement tainted with a slight impatience. I did as requested but again failed to see the point. *"What exactly am I looking for?"* I asked, bemused. *"The boat"* said Ed, excitedly, *"they are pictured as taking to a life boat."*

Ed had dug up some wonderful facts about the *Nancy* packet and its passengers and had a complete grasp on the story. Although fully aware of this, I still only had the everyday basic local modern day knowledge of the wreck in mind. He again went over the text on how the victims had taken to a small boat. He then compared it to how the wreck was then worked by a contemporary professional salvage team; Ed put it clearly as he read out the reference: "*a short distance from the island.*" Ed then paused looking at me expectantly but I just frowned. "*Don't you see?"* he added, *"the ship must have been lost on the Rosevear Ledges."* I looked at him still trying to grasp his thread. "W*hy else would they need to take to a boat, unless they needed it to cross the water, and why would this previously unseen salvage report say that the wreck was - a short distance away from the island - unless in fact it was."* Ed spoke confidently emphasising the key sentences. Assuming his research was correct, and also knowing that it contradicted any modern records we had both read, I'm sure he could physically hear the penny drop. Just to be sure he spelled it out to me again, *"The ship had indeed struck the Gilstone Rock further out as reported but she was then driven onto the Rosevear Ledges and not the island as stated later elsewhere. The survivors onboard the sinking vessel, now wedged firmly on the Rosevear Ledges, had taken to the ship's jolly boat. And this forlorn attempt at survival was then driven onto*

Rosevear island. It was in the capsizing of this small boat where Ann Cargill had met her end and not in the ship as a whole as stated in the limited literature available on Scilly. It was in the confusion between the driving of the ship onto Rosevear Ledges and then the driving of its service boat onto the island, which has kept the position of the Nancy packet an enigma to this day." Feeling a little dim at not having seen what was right in front of me, I still found Ed's animated state really quite infectious. *"What about the treasure?"* I asked, *"are we likely to encounter it?"* At this he did not look so positive. He shuffled his file and produced a few selected pieces of paperwork. *"Well, according to this newspaper report it is unlikely."* He then handed me a facsimile of an article from an old newspaper dated 13th March 1784. It was taken from the Morning Post and disappointingly one sentence read that: *"greater part of the specie brought over in the packet will probably be saved, as the ship remains where she sunk, and can be got at low water."* This was disappointing news but knowing that salvage would have only been undertaken by way of a viewing glass and tools from the surface above the wreck, I angled for something more positive by saying, *"It doesn't necessarily follow that the treasure was actually lifted, after all, the locals' salvage capabilities, although quite good, were rather limited."* I spoke optimistically but Ed had already pre-empted any supposition by handing me another piece of paper. It was his file on the Braithwaites, and it was immediately obvious that the involvement of these professional salvage men was a much more serious occurrence. I read the documents with disappointment and scrutinised every word looking for holes. *"Yes, they had visited the wreck site,"* I said *"but there is no record of them lifting the treasure, or anything else for that matter."*

"No, I must say I haven't unearthed one as yet," said Ed, in agreement, *"but had you been in their shoes and you had lifted money you could readily spend, would you let all and sundry know about it?"* Reluctantly I was forced to agree. It was time to call a meeting of the team and, treasure or not, it wasn't going to take too much to convince the others that this was a project worthy of their best efforts.

And beautiful, midst that wild scene,
Gleamed up the boy's dead face,
like slumbers trustingly serene,
in melancholy grace.

Unknown author

4. Diving Rosevear Ledges

Buccaneer anchored amongst the Rosevear Ledges at low tide

The Rosevear Ledges are a large area of submerged granite that, in thousands of years past, would once have been an extension to Rosevear island itself. Today, the ledges are cut off from the island with the two separate areas divided by a small channel of water. Only the very tops of the ledges can now be seen at low tide; denoted on the surface of the sea by numerous low lying rocks. These rocks, awash at low spring tides, seem to be the very hull-ripping teeth of the ledges but many other rocks still remain unseen beneath the surface, given away by eddies of disturbed water or by a dark patch below the water's surface. Many ships have come to grief on the outer ledges of this reef and although divers had located wrecks in the area in the 1970s, it was the inner ledges where Ed believed we should search for the *Nancy* packet.

That spring we were all itching to get started but due to electrical problems with our boat *Buccaneer,* we did not get onto the water until well into May. As it was to turn out, this was not such a problem as the spring and summer of 2007 was to prove to be wet and windy across not just Scilly but the whole of the United Kingdom. Worse than this, the in-water visibility was awful for an unusually extensive amount of time and did not improve until well into July. This was due to an abnormally large plankton bloom which, on decaying, turned the waters among the Western Rocks white in colour; it would have been like diving into cold semi-skimmed milk. When eventually the dead plankton had moved away from the islands, it was aided on its way by a rough sea. We knew it would take a while for the sea to then be calm enough to dive but regardless of this, in our eagerness to get started, we made numerous attempts to encroach upon the Western Rocks. The first was an uncomfortable event where we knew diving would be impossible but just felt the need to acquaint Ed with the location. We crossed a rough sea to reach the Western Rocks beyond and timidly entered the Neck of Rosevear. Once in this neck we had no option but to progress through as there wasn't enough room to turn our boat around. Half way through we could perceive just how rough the sea was beyond. Now left with no other choice, due to the narrowness of the neck, we continued and eventually emerged at the seaward side of the island. Here we found the open ocean surging and turbulent. Within moments a large wall of water came straight towards the neck, forcing us to immediately turn the boat about. The wheel was put hard over and with the throttle at full power the boat literally surfed back into the neck. Eventually we emerged from the original entrance but not without a huge sigh of relief at not being swamped, or hitting any undesirable obstacles on the way. As a result of conditions like these our target area was unfit to even visit until mid July. During this time we tested our magnetometer equipment and found it needed an overhaul; it was long overdue. A magnetometer picks up disturbances in the earth's magnetic field caused by iron objects on the sea floor. The instrument consists of a display panel connected to a standard car battery and a cable that tows a sensor pulse emitter, or magnetometer fish, through the water. When performing a magnetometer survey it is usually from a large craft like our main boat *Buccaneer* and over relatively deep water. Normally lots of cable is needed to get the magnetometer fish as low to the seabed as possible. However, in very shallow water over an area like the Rosevear Ledges, it is better to suspend the magnetometer fish from a buoy and tow it a short distance behind a non-magnetic craft such as our inflatable rubber punt. With the equipment set up in this way we were all set for the hunt ahead.

When eventually the weather had improved we set off once more, full of expectation, towards the Western Rocks. This time conditions on the Atlantic side of Rosevear were found to be very different from before; on this occasion all was relatively calm and tranquil. As a result we set up the magnetometer equipment on our inflatable punt as planned and, as expected, this allowed us to conduct our survey much closer in amongst the rocks; minimising any danger to our main boat.

Magnetometer set up aboard the punt with the pulse emitter suspended from a buoy astern.

During the survey the equipment picked up one or two targets. We buoyed the spot and then anchored *Buccaneer* in a safe area just down tide from all the rocks. The idea being that the divers could swim over to the buoy during slack water, then search the sea bed for the iron anomalies. They could then emerge from the dive drifting towards the boat and not away from it at the end of the search.

On a still but overcast July afternoon, two team members kitted up for our very first dive. As we did so, Ed advised us not to rely on finding the *Nancy's* anchors or the half a dozen or so small six pound calibre guns, as these, like most of Ann Cargill's personal fortune, had probably been lifted by the Braithwaites months after the wreck took place. However, this was by no means a certainty. With the team prepared to move extremely slowly among the weed fronds, in search of any smaller artefact evidence, we set off towards the nearby rocks looking for what may still remain of the wreck of the *Nancy* packet. Usually in such a search endless dives are needed to be performed but when Ed's research was combined with the magnetometer survey, this proved to be unnecessary. As a result, after only a few dives, the team came upon the scattered remains of an uncharted wreck site at a depth of seventeen metres. The first thing we spotted at the foot of the reef, were two metal rudder gudgeons. Between Ed, myself and the other team members, we had a wealth of experience in the identifying and dating of artefacts found on eighteenth century shipwrecks. Moreover, with both our previous projects being ships lost in that same period, identifying the *Nancy* was going to be right up our street.

Rudder gudgeons are the metal mountings that fit around the stern post of a ship with the purpose of holding the rudder in place. The overall size of these gudgeons were over three feet across; and a stern post of that size pointed emphatically towards them as coming from a medium sized vessel; just the right size for the *Nancy*. The gudgeons were made of iron and as such, most certainly caused one of the anomalies picked up by the magnetometer survey. We now needed to gain an accurate position for these artefacts so that we could strike out from the position in the hope of finding more signs of wreck. For this exercise the divers carried a reel of long thin line with a small yellow buoy attached. This was used to link any wreckage found. It was then further used to mark the water's surface to give the position of anything of significance found on the sea floor. The line was tied to a rudder gudgeon and after our preliminary searches were completed, the marker buoy was attached then sent

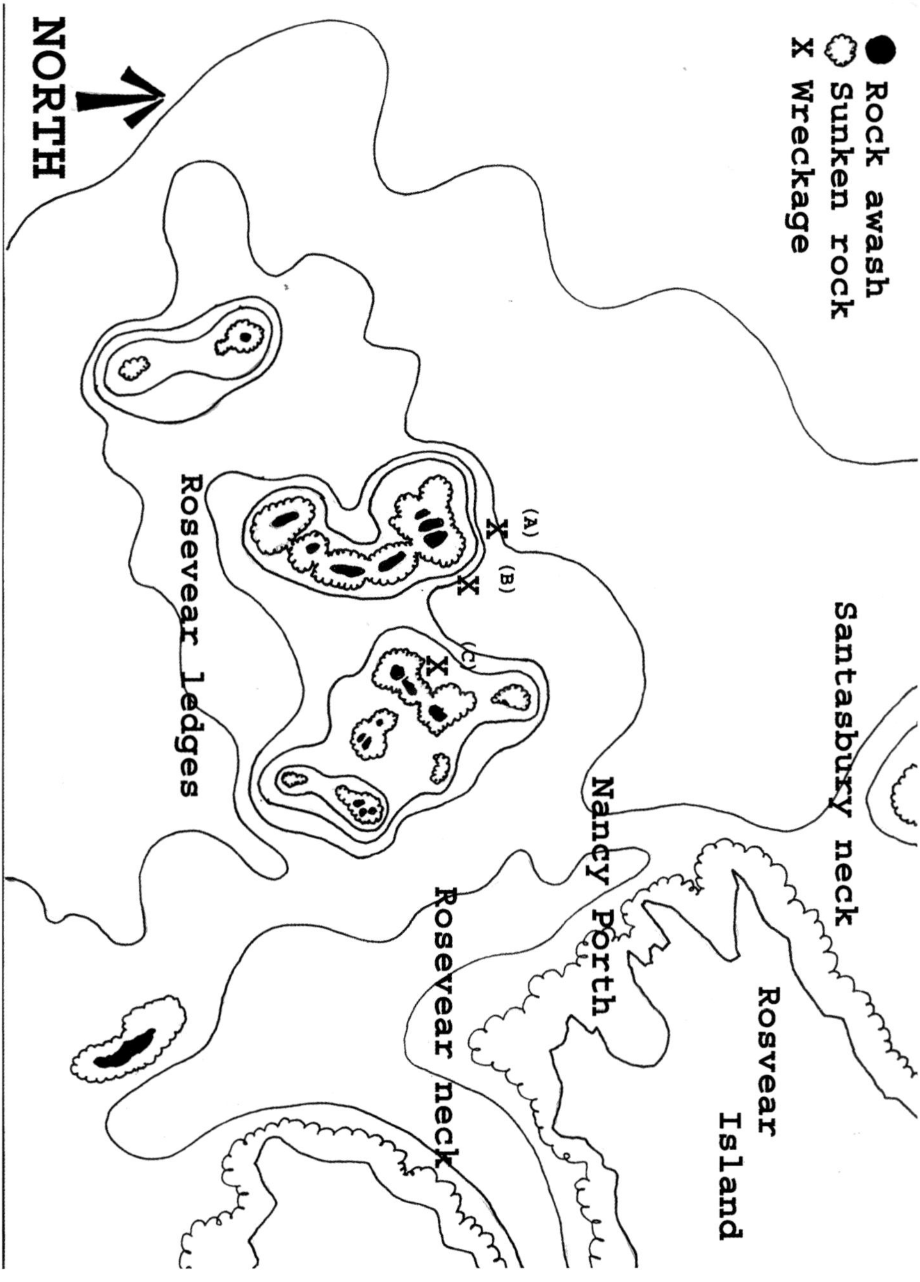

Rosevear Ledges showing areas (A,B &C) of wreckage encountered by the team

up to the surface. We now had a marker to gain an accurate position of our wreck site. Ed as boatman was astonished, if not extremely pleased, to see the marker buoy break the surface on this one of our initial visits to the area.

On later dives we searched around the gudgeons for further wreckage and found evidence of a vessel of the size and age of the *Nancy* packet. We found large ten-inch long copper nails dotted about the site and surrounding an area of sheet lead fragments. As the search area expanded other ironwork, including large iron knees, were also spotted around the site. All this evidence was of significance. The copper nails, for instance, were similar to ones Ed had found on another wreck of an East India Company ship he had worked in the past. Whereas the defined area of sheet lead may have been the lining to the walls of either a small powder magazine, which denoted the wreck as possibly being armed, or the lining of the walls of the hold and used to keep cargo dry during transportation. This would be especially prevalent in a ship that carried mail and despatches. The iron knees we found were also of interest as these were very often used by the East India Company in the construction of its ships during the mid to late eighteenth century. Most other ship builders did not adopt this method of strengthening vessels until well into the nineteenth century.

As the search progressed we also found various fragments of pottery that dated the site to the mid to late eighteenth century. Some of the fragments we found were Chien Lung (The Great Happy Emporer) dynasty originating in China and only made for sale in the Far East. It is well-documented that East India Company ships often carried wares of this kind for use on board ship. We found patterned pieces as well as plain. The blue and white 'Lotus' patterned pieces were used by officers etc, whereas the plain (Qing) ware was for use by the rest of the crew. *(See picture on page 186)*
At a later date team members searched around the shallow areas of the rock nearest our initial finds, where among mainly fragmentary material we encountered a very heavy ship's grinding wheel. Apart

Paul enjoys an unusually calm trip through Rosevear Neck.
Carmen and Phil share a joke during our search for the Nancy.

from any copper nails, the wheel was the only other still completely identifiable artefact found thus far; so we raised it to the surface. Although quite a nice find the wheel was completely useless in the dating and identification of the wrecksite. Over the coming weeks the team further expanded the search to find the wreck was positioned between and over two separate areas of the ledges. Linked by smaller if harder to find artefacts, the site appeared to comprise of three distinct areas of wreckage. Area (A) constituted

Author's wife Carmen Stevens in position over one of the large iron rudder gudgeons in area (A), which possibly indicate the stern area of the wreck site.

Dive brothers Todd and Paul Stevens hold the heavy grinding stone brought up from the wreck site seventeen metres below.
(Photograph by Barbara Cumming)

by far the largest amount of wreckage with three different sized but matching anchors; one sheet anchor, one bower anchor and one kedge anchor. These were surrounded by lots of other material including the rudder gudgeons and numerous iron knees. This is possibly where the ship, after going to pieces, had initially sunk to the bottom. It was also the position of our preliminary discoveries. From experiences gained whilst diving this area it soon became clear that any prevailing sea action, regardless of wind direction, appeared to come from the northwest. Consequently our search, also guided by the trail of wreckage, naturally took us predominantly in a southeasterly direction towards Nancy Porth. Before long we had discovered what we have now come to know as areas (B) & (C) (*See site plans on either page 173 or 187*)

Every dive brought more wreckage hidden beneath boulders and in caves or among the loose rocks and sand. Area (B) at first glance, consisted of one bower anchor and one kedge anchor surrounded by other large iron objects. The presence of large iron anchors was encouraging as it meant that, if this was the *Nancy* packet, then the Braithwaites had not recovered as much as Ed had first assumed. Large anchors, like guns and larger items in general, would have been a main target for any salvage men to lift; especially if like the Braithwaites they were hoping to impress the East India Company in order to gain further salvage contracts. Perhaps we thought, completely understandably, they may have simply filled their pockets with Ann Cargill's money and jewels and left happy and contented with that. Who wouldn't?

The search thus far had been moderately simple since much of the wreckage was found in relatively deep water where constricting weed growth is less prolific. When we had identified a rough

Co author Ed Cumming casts an experienced eye over an artefact from the wreck site.

position in the centre of all this wreckage, the location was chosen as the best place to anchor from then on; it was over the site but not too close to any of the surrounding rocks and suitable for a small craft like *Buccaneer.* Careful anchoring here was crucial, as the boat pivoted on its anchor as and when the tides turned. We did find, however, that from this position the team could strike out in all directions on the seabed to search and return safely from each dive, even though the boat was literally positioned between the proverbial *rock and a hard place*.

Co-Author Todd Stevens tags an iron knee in the shallows; one of many found down on the wrecksite. This one is in area (A).

We saw her proud flag struck that morn,
a star once o'er the seas.
Her helm beat down- her deck uptorn,
And sadder sights than these.
Unknown author

5. Guns and Anchors

Team member James Fletcher gives some scale to one of the Sheet anchors found in area (A). These anchors were just the right style and size to be from the Nancy packet.

Ships of the eighteenth century carried upwards of six anchors, two sheet (or best bower) anchors were the biggest, two bower anchors (or spares) and two small kedge anchors. Anchors produced for English ships between 1750 and 1800 are of a particular type and shape. For instance, the anchors we found had flat-sided iron shafts with short arms supporting extremely large flukes (or palms). They were also wooden-stocked which gave them a date of pre-1810 After that date anchors were produced with iron stocks. Similarly the flat-sided shaft and arms were replaced with completely rounded designs by the early nineteenth century. All these features certainly indicated our site to have been from the mid to late eighteenth century. Thus far we had identified five anchors of this type on our site, possibly leaving us with at least one more to find. We certainly hoped to find some small calibre guns.

The weather during August and September allowed us to continue with our search. During this time we came across more iron knees bringing the count to seven and numerous other large iron objects such as spars, braces and stretchers. One of the knees was found, along with many other iron objects, to be hidden in caves on the north and eastern side of the rocks in area (C). Without the need to perform any excavation work, we also found evidence of copper sheathing, fragments of teak wood, iron shot and evidence of musket flints. With all the evidence emerging pointing towards our quarry, Ed was becoming convinced that we had indeed found the site of the *Nancy* packet. We took measurements and photographs and got expert help to identify and date of some of the smaller artefacts like the pottery.

Everything pointed towards the *Nancy, "but where were her guns and the treasure?"* I kept asking. *"The Braithwaites,"* replied Ed each and every time. Being a profound optimist I was still not convinced, so looked more closely at the site plan we were producing. We had searched all around the north side of the rocks in area (A); similarly the expanse of seabed between areas (A) & (C), which lead us to discover areas (B) & (C) respectively. Where to look next was the question. The wreckage found so far had been well spread over a distance of about one hundred and fifty metres, some of it hidden in caves in area (C). Perhaps it was spread even further still towards Rosevear island, so we set off to hunt around the eastern side of the rocks of that area. During one dive in that position we found yet another iron knee to the south of the rocks. The knee gave us hope to continue as it exactly matched all the others bringing the knee count to eight in total. *"OK,"* I said to the others, spurred on by the discovery of the latest knee, *"I think we should do a systematic search of the whole south side of the rocks of area (C)".* This statement was understandably met with incredulity, as the weed we had just encountered there was incredibly thick. As a result I elected to do this part of the search; the theory being a single diver could move much faster alone. *"How will you know what areas you have covered?"* asked Carmen knowing just how thick the weed was, *"the whole seabed looks the same."* she added. Carmen's concern was

Carmen places a gloved hand on one of the knees found in a cave in area (C)

completely reasonable and that night, after a little thought, I came up with the answer. On our next trip out to the wreck I took along a sharp hatchet. The plan was to move gradually east to west along the reef, in channels no more than ten feet apart, that went north to south. North went up the reef's side with south obviously being down. Then, using depth of water and the sun to guide me along, I cut down kelp in channels to mark where I had been. The scheme worked perfectly and we discovered two small guns as a result. The trouble now was that we needed to positively link the guns and area (C) together with the rest of the wreckage. We had found knees on either side of the guns but these were quite a distance away. We had also found wreckage on all sides of the reef in area (C). However, something else much closer to the guns needed to be found to complete the link. The only area not yet searched was the most dangerous; and it was up and over the very top of the ledges. This is one of the only times when shallow diving can be just as dangerous as diving in deep water. To accomplish this part of the search we needed a long sustained period of calm weather, otherwise the surge crashing over the rocks was too strong to fight against. Such a calm period had not yet occured that season. In fact, it wasn't until into mid September that we finally got even the remotest chance to perform this part of the search.

To all intents and purposes the sea in September became as calm as we could possibly hope for. Consequently, moving around the rocks very close to the surface, Carmen and I were buffeted about by the surge. Worse than this, when one enters into a shallow underwater crevice or channel in the rock, the surge sucks the diver in or out or throws him or her around at the sea's mercy. This type of dive usually involves lots of holding on tight to weed fronds, cracks and fissures or wedging oneself between the rocks. Although very shallow, this type of diving is not for the faint hearted. During one such dive we moved carefully among the rocks trying to stay on track in the surge. We moved up the reef from the south and went over the very top, all the while attempting to hold on tight whenever feeling the sea's push and pulling motion. At one point we reached a large cleft in the summit. Here we could either be sucked right over the reef top by the surge or we could retreat back away down the reef the way we came. Perceiving a clear run through the gap we elected the former. We let go of the rock at the right moment and let the sea drag us through the cleft. The bottom and sides of the cleft flashed by in an instant and we were forcibly ejected out the other side of the reef. As we went we passed over a large iron object protruding from a tight opening in the reef's side. We turned and gingerly went back up for a second look, all the while holding on tight as the sea moved over us. When we reached a place where we could again view the object, we were amazed to find it to be another large sheet anchor. Not only that, this very large iron artefact had somehow managed to become positioned into a seemingly impossible situation. Incredibly, almost the whole anchor was completely lodged in a very tight crack in the rock which was only just wide enough to accept it. We also found other items of wreckage close by this anchor. Two things about the anchor pleased us immensely. Firstly it was identical in style and size to the other anchors we had found in areas (A) & (B); and secondly it was within reasonably close proximity to the small guns I had found earlier. This pointed towards all the wreckage we had seen so far as being from the same shipwreck. But was this the wreck of the *Nancy* packet? A question that could only be answered with the discovery of something more positively identifiable; something belonging to an individual like Ann Cargill, or property of the East India Company and bearing its unique insignia.

The author rests by one of the guns found after a difficult search in thick kelp, which was then cut down for the photograph

The guns we had found were small and of a size that we were hoping to find. Sadly though, other than being the correct calibre, the guns were too corroded to enable us to glean any further information. If we had seen ten in number that would have helped greatly but so few were found on the wreck site. We could only conjecture that this was due to salvage. Only the East India archives may show whether or not the Braithwaites had been paid for lifting iron guns from the *Nancy*. However, that particular research could turn out to be a lengthy and very expensive exercise. The problem with living somewhere as remote as Scilly, is that research becomes extremely expensive and we had spent more than enough money on the project already. Although the enterprise had thus far been an enjoyable voyage of discovery, without return, our financial limits had been reached; signalling an imminent end to the season's project. Although it would be easy to say that, given all the evidence found so far, we had located the *Nancy*, the facts dictate that at present the wreck would actually have to remain as unidentified.

(Top) Chien Lung Dynasty lotus pattern bowl fragments (Bottom) Qing bowl fragments. All were found on the wrecksite in Area (C)
(Photograph by Ed Cumming)

The site plan on the opposite page is a scaled down representation of a more detailed drawing of the wreck-site. The original drawing is held in the archives of the Isles of Scilly Museum. The National Monuments Records Office also hold a copy.

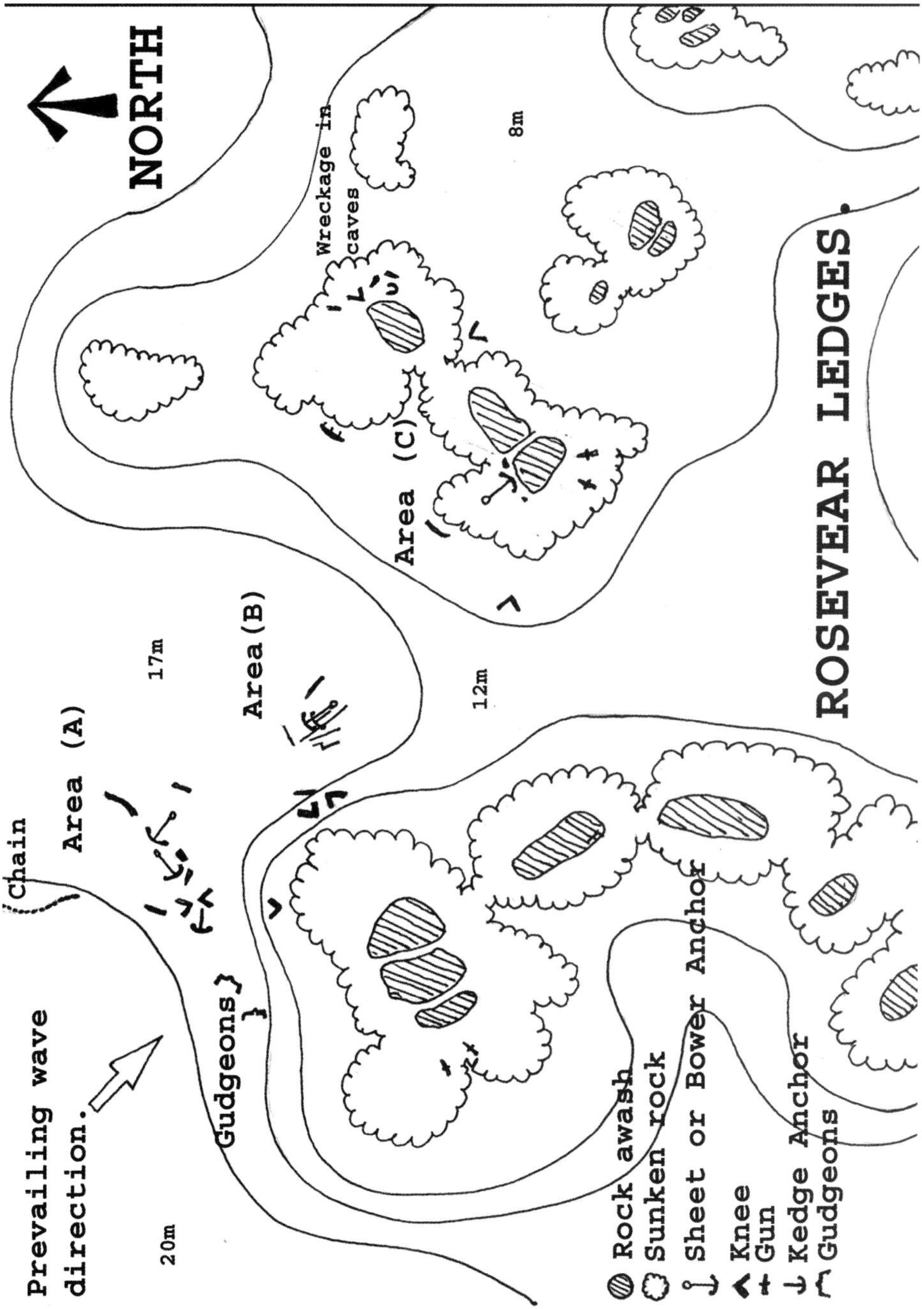
NORTH
Prevailing wave direction.
20m
Area (A)
Chain
17m
Area (B)
12m
Gudgeons
Area (C)
Wreckage in caves
8m
ROSEVEAR LEDGES.
Rock awash
Sunken rock
Sheet or Bower Anchor
Knee
Gun
Kedge Anchor
Gudgeons

And near him on the sea weed lay,
Till then we had not wept,
but well our gushing hearts might say,
that there a mother slept.

Unknown author

6. Old Town Revisted

Alfred Trenear and Father Guy Scott just prior to the service
(Photograph by Chris Hall)

The team had derived an enormous amount of pleasure from the project thus far and felt it was time to give something back. This kind of action is often achieved by giving the local museum a display of artefacts raised. Unfortunately, apart from a stone grinding wheel, some shards of broken pottery, and a few odd bits and bobs, we had nothing more of any great interest to give. Ed and I racked our brains but could only think of continuing to search the wrecksite next season, in the hopes of finding something more worthwhile for display. However, when on one windy day Ed and I visited the Church in Old Town on St Mary's Island, hoping to find clues to the siting of the reported '*neat monument*' to Ann Cargill, we were inadvertently presented with the perfect scenario.

Built on the site of a Norman 12th century church, the modern church is a modest but beautiful little granite structure, with a small open belfry in which swings a single small brass bell. The church is set in amongst a small area of trees and stands on the western side of Old Town Bay on a gentle slope overlooking the sea. Like something out of an old horror movie, many of its old gravestones either leaning over or standing at random angles. Within the church grounds there are many unmarked graves harbouring shipwreck victims now long forgotten. However, there is a large monument that stands in a prominent position to remind everyone of the *Schiller* disaster in 1875. The victims names are not shown but many are buried beneath the very long walkway that leads up towards the church door. The churchyard holds countless other shipwreck victims and somewhere in the grounds, probably to the south of the church, is the grave of Ann Cargill. For hours Ed and I searched among the gravestones hoping to find the marker for Ann's final resting place but were disappointed to discover that it no longer existed. This was a shame as her grave would have been a very tangible link with our project. Furthermore, through our researching and writings, we had both become immersed in Ann's life and naturally harboured vague feelings of having known her personally. As a result we immediately knew what to do. Replacing some form of memorial would be the perfect way of putting things to rights. Consequently we sought a meeting with the local Parish Priest, Father Guy Scott, in the hope of gaining his permission to replace a suitable memorial to Ann Cargill and the *Nancy* packet victims.

Taking the story of Ann Cargill along to the meeting, as proof that the *'neat monument'* had once existed, I presented Father Scott with our team's proposal. Fully expecting a negative response, or at very least presented with forms to fill in. A short conversation later brought the pleasant surprise of complete agreement to the proposal. There were however a couple of provisos, one being that the local undertaker Alfred Trenear also sanctioned the idea, and that the replacement could only be placed after efforts had been taken to identify where the original grave was originally positioned.

Alfred Trenear is a tall thin elderly gentleman with a trim white beard and moustache. He is friendly and approachable and can often be seen riding his pushbike about the island. I was already acquainted with Alfie and knew that, like Ed and myself, he appreciated anything to do with island history. After an amenable meeting with Alfie at his home, he also agreed to our proposal of a new modest memorial to Ann Cargill and the victims of the *Nancy* packet. He then searched his archives to see where Ann's original grave may have been sited but unfortunately these records no longer existed. Alfred did, however, identify a general area in the churchyard where the original tombstone may once have stood. As expected, he believed it would have been south of the church.

At a later date Alfred, Father Scott and I met at the churchyard and a spot was chosen for the plaque. Eventually, the day came to place it and everyone involved went along to the ceremony. Gathered around the spot Father Scott, Ed and myself said a few words to the *Nancy* packet victims; it was very poignant. To Ed, myself and the rest of the team, it was also fitting that someone once so famous and interesting was allowed to be remembered, if only in this modest way.

Ed starts the modest service with a few words about the victims of the Nancy packet. After reading out all the poems associated with the wreck, Ed and I realised just how involved we had become in the story; it was a very touching moment for all present.

(Photograph by Chris Hall)

Oh, human love! Whose yearning heart
though all things vainly true,
so stamps up on thy mortal part,
its passionate adieu!
Unknown author

7. The Grave on Rosevear Island

Ed's wife Barbara waves to the authors as we head off to explore Rosevear Island.

Ann Cargill's last resting place on St Mary's was not the end of the story as regards links with her and the victims of the *Nancy* packet; we had two more places to search.

Ed had unearthed an important, if distant, link to the wreck in the grounds of Duddingston Parish Church in Edinburgh Scotland. In March 1784 the last will and testament of Captain John Haldane was read with part of it stating that he had left two hundred pounds for building a memorial to his grandfather. Erected in 1788, this monument still stands in the Duddingston churchyard to this day. One side of it is dedicated to Patrick Haldane John's grandfather who, after the death of his father, had become john's only parent. Interestingly, and as a pleasant surprise to Ed and I, on the reverse side of the monument there is a large marble relief which was dedicated to John Haldane. It was placed there by his friends after he died in the *Nancy* packet disaster. The relief is of a small ship being wrecked on a stormy sea; a jolly boat is pictured in the foreground. In the jolly boat one can just make out what looks to be a woman clutching a baby.(*See drawing on page 121*)

During a very calm autumn spell the team set off for the Western Rocks for the last time that season, taking plenty of food along, intent on spending the whole day in the area diving on the wreck site and landing on Rosevear Island. Between dives and after lunch, Ed and I left our partners relaxing on the boat, took the punt and ventured onto Rosevear to explore. Taking a camera along we hoped to take photographic evidence to record anything left by all the past human interaction. We certainly wanted to visit the remains of the cottage still so clearly visible from the sea but hoped to find more; we were not to be disappointed. The cottage stood proudly behind its protective stone on its seaward side, its gables, walls, windows and doorway all still very evident. But to our surprise there were many other things to be found hidden in the surrounding brush or left by visible scarring on the rocks. Apart from the extensive remains of the lighthouse builders' cottage there were the tumbledown walls of a workshop and the solid dressed granite base of where the smithy used to stand. There was a second dressed granite platform, which probably served as the base for a tool-shed. There was also evidence of a walkway and steps that went down to the sea. There was evidence of mooring points, so that a boat could be kept alongside the island; held in position by fixing points in Rosevear Neck and even evidence of a possible landing-stage. After a good look around I climbed to the highest point of the island to where James Douglass used to sit and play his flute. From this lofty position one could see every rock hidden amidst the greenery. Surveying the area south-west of the cottage I could see an odd looking structure that we had not noticed and that did not look to be at all natural. *"What's that, Ed?"* I shouted from on top of the carn. *"What are you looking at?" asked* Ed curiously. Then, staying in this high position, I proceeded to guide Ed towards the spot. He slowly waded his way through the mallow shrubs listening to directions until he was immediately over the feature. He then bent down amongst the overgrown indigenous plant life and started to look more closely at the structure hidden therein. He seemed to take an age to say what it was, so, somewhat impatiently, I called *"What is it then Ed?"*. He looked at it a little more then stood up

and shouted *"Todd, you're not going to believe this, but I think it's a grave."*
I couldn't believe my ears, so asked just to make sure. *"Did you say it's a grave Ed?"*
"Yes," he replied emphatically, *"I can't think of anything else it could possibly be."* This was unbelievable news considering we had gone

The possible grave which is generally obscured by thick tree mallows which grow prolifically during the summer months on Rosevear island.

there hoping to see such archaeology, and with that I rushed down from the carn to join Ed by the strange granite feature. Once at the spot I looked over the object of interest. Clearly denoted by a mound of rocks it certainly looked like a grave and with what appeared to be a large headstone at one end, there was nothing else we thought it could be. Moreover, once we had both examined the feature more closely, we found marks on the headstone clearly showing it to have been cut with the use of hand tools. *"I wish we could tell how old it was,"* I said convinced it was a grave and knowing Ed was thinking the same but further than this he came up with a perfectly reasonable theory for its age. *"Well,"* he said, his forehead furrowed from frowning with deep thought, *"I'm thinking this feature must surely be contemporary with the lighthouse construction workers.""Funnily enough, Ed, that's what I was hoping*

but how can you possibly tell?" I asked thinking the discovery was too good to be true.
"See these marks," replied Ed, running his fingers over a few mysterious grooves in the headstone, *"Yes,"* I said looking more closely, "*Well who other than stone masons would have taken stone cutting tools onto Rosevear,"* he explained confidently. Ed was right, the fact that the stone had been cut must surely have been the efforts of someone like the lighthouse workmen. *"I wonder if the stone is indigenous granite to the islands,"* said Ed thinking still further, *"or is it Lamorna granite, which was brought in for use in the construction of the lighthouse,"* he added. Neither of us could tell which it was, as clearly a test was required to determine this. However, it was a good point which could give a more positive erection date of the structure. Either way, to us, the grave was tangible evidence pointing towards the legend being true; the lighthouse workmen had indeed made a grave for human remains; found by James Douglass in the vegetable patch. We returned to the boat extremely pleased with our visit to Rosevear, although at first our partners, Carmen and Barbara, couldn't quite understand our excitement. To Ed and I the presence of the grave tied in with all our work and gave credence to the Rosevear island legend.

After completing the day's diving we set out the things for tea. With no other vessels evident in the area, we had the Western Rocks to ourselves and relaxed on the boat enjoying the solitude and talking about Rosevear. The sun then began to sink behind the Bishop Rock Lighthouse towards the horizon. Inevitably, the temperature began to drop and the birds suddenly fell silent. We then noticed that all the rocks surrounding us started to take on an orange glow, created by the gradual dimming of the setting sun. Innumerable black shadows created by the many cracks and fissures within the granite gradually grew ever longer. From Pednathise Head in the south to little Crebawethan in the north, with this black and orange hue, these islets reflected the sun's movement across the sky, all encased in a sea with the appearance of undulating mercury. It was all so very tranquil with not a splash of water to be heard on the nearby rocky shores. As we were absorbing the silence and beauty of our surroundings, the seals started to wail their eerie melody. This haunting sound that gently echoed around the rocks turned the natural ambience of the area into something rather eerie. This was only added to by the circumstances of the story for which we had come there in the first place. One's gaze then naturally turned towards the deep lush green upper slopes of Rosevear island, with thoughts given to the victims of the *Nancy* packet still buried therein. Today it appeared an astoundingly beautiful final resting-place for the forgotten victims to be, but then seldom are conditions as good as they were this day among the Western Rocks.

With our surroundings inexorably turning our thoughts towards things of a supernatural nature, we began to conjecture over why Ann Cargill's ghost is supposed to haunt Rosevear. None of us actually believed in such things, nevertheless, we speculated over the reasons why it is so perceived. Firstly, she died here under traumatic circumstances and was originally buried on the island along with her son and lover; and all were buried in unconsecrated ground. She was then exhumed from her resting place and possibly even separated from those she loved and with whom she had perished. As a result one can easily understand why it is believed that Ann Cargill haunts Rosevear. As for actually hearing her ghostly voice singing a lullaby, we heard nothing; only the seals wailing hauntingly across the sea at the setting sun. But who knows, perhaps the circumstances were not conducive enough for Ann to make an appearance. Maybe one day someone else will visit this unique place under the right conditions, perhaps then they will be lucky enough to become the latest audience to hear the beautiful voice of Ann Cargill giving a free performance around Rosevear island. Let's hope so. And what more romantic legend could any place possibly be blessed with.

Lullaby of Rosevear

By

Todd Stevens

Look not beyond these arms my child,
fear not the waves so high.
Mother will keep you safe from harm,
and the tempest wild awry.

Cradling thy head against my breast,
perceive not the deathly crack,
of timbers of the ship's great hull,
upon the Gilstone stack.

Stir not upon the Captain's calls,
the crew his tasks perform.
Keep your eyes to me my boy,
not o'er the water's foam.

A lullaby for you to hear,
a soothing tune- to calm us both.
Tho' the water's cold around my feet,
still my song belies the truth.

Bundled in a coverlet,
for there's no time to dress,
convey you to the jolly boat,
to flee the sea's ingress.

This song I sing my baby boy,
disguises horrors all around,
the death; the pain; the reaper's call;
the breaking ship upon the ground.

Ever louder I hum to thee, my dear
as our boat to shore doth go,
through maelstrom; eddies and whirlpools,
to risk violent surf and undertow.

Pressed close against my bosom child,
you'll not be yielded from my grasp.
Tho' land appears so close at hand,
still I fear we've breathed our last.

A lullaby- the last we'll know,
of this life, this love, this Earth;
for our boat it doth turn over love,
to entomb us in the surf.

So close Rosevear our saving grace,
yet our grave it will become,
interred among the mallow shrubs
with -Haldane- Gleneagle's son.

Lonely Island on the western front,
deserving of a tome,
thy shores be haunted with my song,
from now- 'til kingdom come.

Also by these authors:

Wreck of Colossus
The find of a lifetime.

A book by Todd Stevens
(ISBN: 978 0 955343018)
www.hmscolossus.co.uk

A Dorset Trilogy
(ISBN: 978 0 952410434)
&
Nancy Packet
(ISBN: 978 0 952410441)
Interactive historical CD's by Ed Cumming.
www.weymouthdiving.co.uk

Bibliography

1 - *Nancy* packet Historical Record. ISBN 0-9542104-4-1, Ed Cumming.
2 - Memoirs of the Life of John Philip Kemble Esq., including a history of the stage, from the time of the Garrick to the present period. James Boaden Esq. Pages 85 to 86. Published by Robert H Small & Wilder & Campbell, New York, 1825.
3 - Baldwin, Olive and Thelma Wilson. "Ann Cargill," in Matthew, H. C. G. and Brian Harrison, eds. The Oxford Dictionary of National Biography (ODNB). Vol. 10, pages 93-94. London: 200.
4 - The Gentleman's Magazine and Historical Chronicle, Vol. LIV, For the year MDCCLXXXIV. Sylvanus Urban.
5 - Thomas Williams, The life of Sir James Nicholas Douglass 1900.
6 - Notes & queries by William John Thomas et al. "Ann Cargill was Lauetta in Sheridan's short farce of St Patrick's Day; or The Scheming Lieutenant on its production at Covent Garden on May 2nd 1775."
7 - Peter Patrick Reed, Dissertation. 'Arrant Beggars: Staging the Atlantic Lumpenproletariat 1777 - 1852, Florida State University.
8 - Philip H. Highfill, Kalman A. Burnim and Edward A. Langhams eds. A Biographical Dictionary of Actors, Actresses, Musicians, Dancers, Managers & Other Stage Personnel in London 1600-1800, 16 Volumes (Carbondale: Southern Illinois UP. (1973) 3.65.
9 - Rosevear: A desert island story. Glynis Cooper. Copyright Historic Occasions, ISBN 1 900 00600 6.
10 - The Scillonian Magazine, No. 23, Vol.4, Sept. 1930, page 383. Extracted from Messrs Tonkin's Guide Book.
11 - G. W. Stone, ed., The London Stage, 1660–1800, pt 4: 1747–1776 (1962)
12 - C. B. Hogan, ed., The London Stage, 1660–1800, pt 5: 1776–1800 (1968)
13 - Ships, Shipwrecks and Maritime Incidents around the Isles of Scilly, Museum Publication No. 3, ISBN 0-9523971-4-5.
14 - Recollections of R. J. S. Stevens: an organist in Georgian London, ed. M. Argent (1992).

15 - A Survey of the Ancient and Present State of the Scilly Islands, John Troutbeck, Chaplain to his Grace the Duke of Leeds. Sherbourne, Printed and sold by Goadby and Lerpiniere. Sold by F & C Rivington. No. 62 St Pauls, Church-yard, London, 1796.
16 - Histories of the tête-à-tête annexed, or, Memoirs of the combustible lover, and the eloped Clara, Town and Country Magazine, 8 (1776), 9–11.
17 - Biographical sketch of Miles Peter Andrews, Esq., M.P.', Monthly Mirror (April 1797), 195–200.
18 - M. D. Wells, Memoirs of the life of Mrs Sumbel, late Wells, 3 vols. (1811).
19 - Pasquin [J. Williams], 'The children of Thespis', Poems, 2 [1789].
20 - The letters of Richard Brinsley Sheridan, ed. C. Price, 3 vols. 1966.
21 - Memoirs of William Hickey, ed. A. Spencer, 2 (1918), page 166.
22 - The Memoirs of William Hickey Vol. 2, 1775 - 1782, 'A Dinner on the Britannia', page 166. Mr William Hornby, Governor of Bombay 1771 to 1784
23 - Memoirs of William Hickey, ed. A. Spencer, 2 (1918), pages 170-171.
24 - The diary of Sylas Neville, 1767–1788, ed. B. Cozens-Hardy (1950).
25 - Shipwrecks around the Isles of Scilly (1988), Isles of Scilly Museum.
26 - "ST. HELENA RECORDS" 1673 to 1835.) A work by Hudson Ralph Janisch Esq, a Governor of Jamaica. Compiled by Benjamin Grant in 1885.
27 - A History of the Island of St. Helena, from its Discovery by the Portuguese to the Year 1806. T H Brooke, Black, Parry & Kingsbury, London. 1808 (2nd Ed 1824).
28 - Genealogy information: The Haldanes of Gleneagles by J Aylmer Haldane, Printed Edinburgh; W Blackwood & Sons, 1929.
29 - Annual Register, March 1784, A view of the History, Politics & Literature. 1784-1785, Second edition, London. Printed by J Crowder, Warwick Square, 1800.
30 - The Chronological Historian for 1784 by William Toone, Published in 1826, London, Messrs Longman, Rees, Orme, Brown and Green.

31 - 'Observations on a Current That Often Prevails to the Westward of Scilly; endangering the Safety of Ships that approach the British Channel'. by James Rennell, Esq. Philosophical Transactions of the Royal Society of London, Vol. 83, 1793, p182-200.
32 - Robert Maybee, The Scillonian poet. Isles of Scilly Museum 1973.
33 - Joseph Mackie; The geology of the Isles of Scilly, published in 1858.
34 - Minutes of the Institute of Civil Engineers 1881-1882.
35 - Minutes of the Trinity House annual banquet 1885.
36 - Bishop Rock by Martin Boyle ISBN 1-901043-05-3.

NEWSPAPERS

Morning Post (6 Dec 1775)	Gazetteer (19 Aug 1780)
Morning Post (7 Dec 1775)	Morning Herald (13–14 Sept 1781)
Morning Post (15 Dec 1775)	Morning Herald (26 Sept 1782)
Morning Post (5 Jan 1776)	Morning Herald 8–10 March 1784
Morning Post (5 Oct 1776)	Public Advertiser (1 Aug 1780)
Morning Post (7–9 Oct 1776	Public Advertiser (9 Aug 1780)
Morning Post (24 April 1780)	Public Advertiser (1 Dec 1781)
Morning Post (9 March 1784)	Public Advertiser (8 March 1784)
Morning Post (13 March 1784)	Public Advertiser (10 March 1784)
Morning Chronicle (15 Dec 1775)	Whitehall Evening Post (9 March 1784)
Morning Chronicle (16 Dec 1775)	London Chronicle (9 Aug 1781)
Morning Chronicle (29 Dec 1775)	London Chronicle (6 March 1784)
Morning Chronicle (7 Oct 1776)	London Chronicle (9 March 1784)
Morning Chronicle (9 Aug 1781)	London Chronicle (11 March 1784)
Morning Chronicle (13 Sept 1781)	Bath Chronicle (11 March 1784)
Morning Chronicle (15 Sept 1781)	Times (6 November 1947)
Morning Chronicle (8 March 1784)	Times (29 January 1913)
Morning Chronicle (9 March 1784)	Courtesy of the Oxford Dictionary of National Biography (ODNB)

Poems

Untitled - *Nancy* packet disaster poem by unknown author.
The Poetical Album and Register of Modern Fugitive Poetry.

All night the booming minute-gun
had peeled along the deep'
and mournfully the rising sun,
looked o'er the tide worn steep.

A Bark from India's coral strand'
before the rushing blast'
had veiled her top sails to the sand,
and bowed her noble mast.

The queenly ship!-brave hearts had striven,
and true ones died with her!
We saw her mighty cable riven,
like floating gossamer!

We saw her proud flag struck that morn,
a star once o'er the seas,
Her helm beat down her deck uptorn,
and sadder things than these!

Her sails were draggled in the brine,
that gladdened late the skies,
and her pennon, that kissed the fair moonshine
down many a fathom lies.

We saw her treasures cast away;
the rocks with pearl were sown;
and strangely sad, the ruby's ray
flashed out o'er the fretted stone.

And gold was strewn the wet sands o'er
like ashes by a breeze,
and gorgeous robes, but oh! that shore
had sadder sights than these.

We saw the strong man, still and low,
a crushed reed thrown aside!
Yet, by that rigid lip and brow,
not with out strife he died!

And near him on the sea-weed lay
till then we had not wept,
but well our gushing hearts might say
that there a mother slept.

For her pale arms a babe had passed
with such a wreathing grasp'
billows had dashed o'er that fond breast
yet not undone the clasp!

Her very trussess had been flung
to wrap the child's fair form,
where still their wet, long streamers clung'
all tangled by the storm.

And beautiful, 'midst that wild scene,
gleamed up the boys dead face,
like slumbers trustingly serene,
in melancholy grace.

Deep in her bossom lay his head,
with half shut violet eye;
he had known little of her dread,
nought of her agony!

Oh! human love! whose yearning heart,
through all things vainly true,
so stamps up on thy mortal part,
its passionate adieu!

Surely thou hast another lot'
there is some home for thee,
where thou shalt rest, remembering not,
the moaning of the sea!

Untitled - *Nancy* packet disaster poem possibly by Robert Maybee?
A copy of verses made upon the untimely death of the beautiful Mrs. Cargill.
Madden Ballads.

Dismal is the tale
which I now unto you relate.
Hearts which are not cold to beauty,
must lament a fair ones fate.

Cargill ,who did rival venus,
now alas! will charm no more.
Each rose and lily now is faded,
wrecked near Scilly's fatal shore.

This fair one she from England sailed,
bound to India's golden shore,
from friends, relations, then she parted,
but little thought to meet no more.

With spreading canvas in the Ocean,
swift the vessel sailed along,
safe conveyed to the Indies,
the queen of beauty dance and song.

Golden treasure there she gained,
numerous charms soon drew a throng,
hearts were conquered by her beauty,
ears delighted with her song.

Longing for to see old England,
she prepared for to depart,
aboard the Nancy took her passage,
with heavy purse and lighted heart.

Cheerful gales her ship directed,
soon they thought to view our shore,
but alas! the fates ordained,
England they must see no more.

On cursed Scilly's dreadful rocks,
Neptune then their vessel tossed,
she foundered split and went to pieces,
every soul on board were lost.

Pen or tongue scarce can describe,
the horrors of that dreadful night,
these poor souls saw death before them,
in every form that can affright.

Scarce had time unto the Lord to pray,
that he their souls would save,
ere the vessel went to pieces,
and they found a watery grave.

Drove to land by foaming billow,
on shore was found poor Cargill's clay.
Clasped within her lifeless arms,
her tender infant then it lay.

To one grave they were committed,
Scilly's earth on them was cast.
Cargill will no more delight us,
these fleeting pleasures now are past.

So peace be to her precious soul,
tho' dreadful was her timeless fate,
we hope the Lord her sins forgave
and now she is in blessed state.

Different ways grim death attacks us,
youth and age before him fall.
Let everyone prepare to meet him,
none can tell when he will call.